Becoming the System

Oxford Studies in Language and Race is an interdisciplinary forum that positions issues of race, racism, and racialization as central to language-based scholarship. The series publishes leading, state-of-the-art research in the field of language and race, broadly construed, and considers the complexities of language and race both historically and within rapidly changing politics, demographic shifts, migrations, and technological advances of the 21st century. As the study of language and race continues to take on a growing importance across anthropology, communication studies, cultural studies, education, linguistics, literature, psychology, race and ethnic studies, sociology, and other fields, this series represents a timely and urgently needed effort to focus these fields on the central role that language plays in the enduring relevance of race, racism, and racialization in the lives of racially minoritized populations both within and beyond the United States.

Becoming the System

A Raciolinguistic Genealogy of Bilingual Education in the Post–Civil Rights Era

NELSON FLORES

OXFORD
UNIVERSITY PRESS

Oxford University Press is a department of the University of Oxford. It furthers the University's objective of excellence in research, scholarship, and education by publishing worldwide. Oxford is a registered trade mark of Oxford University Press in the UK and certain other countries.

Published in the United States of America by Oxford University Press
198 Madison Avenue, New York, NY 10016, United States of America.

CIP data is on file at the Library of Congress

ISBN 978–0–19–751682–9 (pbk.)
ISBN 978–0–19–751681–2 (hbk.)

DOI: 10.1093/oso/9780197516812.001.0001

Paperback printed by Marquis Book Printing, Canada
Hardback printed by Bridgeport National Bindery, Inc., United States of America

Contents

Contents

Acknowledgments

It is a bit overwhelming to sit down and write an acknowledgments section to this book since in many ways it has taken my entire life to get here. It was growing up in a low-income bilingual Latinx household in Philadelphia before being transported to Swarthmore College and then back to Philadelphia and then New York City as an ESL teacher that provided the foundation for the journey that would lead me to writing this book. It was pursuing doctoral work at the CUNY Graduate Center and then going through the tenure track at the University of Pennsylvania where this foundation became nurtured and encouraged to grow. To name everybody that has supported me along the way would take more pages than the length of this book. So I wanted to start by giving a general thank you to everybody who has helped me to get to where I am today. That being said, there are some key people who have supported me in my journey to this point who I would also like to personally acknowledge.

I really could not have gotten to this point without the strong support that I received from the faculty in the Educational Studies program at Swarthmore College. Eva Travers supervised my senior thesis on the politics of bilingual education and school choice in the School District of Philadelphia and her spirit lives on in this book. Lisa Smulyan first introduced me to the power of deconstruction with the goal of imagining new possibilities that provided the first kernels of what would become raciolinguistic genealogy. Swarthmore is also where I met my academic soulmate Jonathan Rosa who has been my ride or die for so many years now. I could not imagine having done any of this without him.

My time in the Urban Education program at the CUNY Graduate Center has also shaped this book in innumerable ways. Words cannot begin to express how grateful I am to Ofelia García who not only pushed me in my thinking but also nurtured me in ways that have encouraged me to embrace my outsider status and to see it as my biggest strength. I am also so grateful to having had the opportunity to work with Jean Anyon whose spirit lives on in my insistence on the importance of addressing broader political and economic factors in educational reform. Ricardo Otheguy has been such a model for how to push students in their thinking in ways that build them up rather than tear them down, which is a model I try to emulate with my own students. I am also so grateful for having had the opportunity to conduct research under the supervision of Kate Menken and Tatyana Kleyn whose critical reflective stance toward the classification of Long term English learner opened up space for us to collaboratively build a critique that provided the foundation for the critique of the category that I further develop in this book. I am a better scholar for having had the opportunity to work with all of these amazing mentors.

I have also had the great fortune to work with amazing colleagues in Educational Linguistics at the University of Pennsylvania. Betsy Rymes chaired the search that hired me and has been a great mentor, supporter, and collaborator ever since. Nancy Hornberger was generous enough to share with me some of the materials that she had collected over the years in her own work in the School District of Philadelphia with some of those materials appearing in the book. Our newest faculty member María Cioè-Peña continues to inspire me in the ways that she has taken up a raciolinguistic perspective in new and exciting ways.

I have also had the opportunity to work with so many amazing students at the University of Pennsylvania who have shaped my thinking in so many ways. I would like to give special shoutouts to Aldo Anzures-Tapia, Sofia Chaparro, Frances Kvietok Dueñas, Mark Lewis, Lauren McAuliffe, Jennifer Phuong, and Karla Venegas for their support of the Philadelphia Bilingual Education Project that provided foundational research that informed this book.

I also wanted to thank several organizations that have supported my research across the years. The School District of Philadelphia provided funding to support the Philadelphia Bilingual Education Project in conducting research on dual language education in the district that is discussed in this book. The National Academy of Education selected me for a 2017 NAED/Spencer postdoctoral fellowship that provided me with the much needed time to do the archival work necessary for completing this book. The Spencer Foundation has also supported my work in others ways including through support a conference that I organized with Uju Anya and Tia Madkins entitled "Centering Black Students in Language Education" that pushed me in my thinking about the relationship between anti-Blackness and Latinidad that helped to shape this book and through commissioning me to write a white paper on culturally sustaining and relevant education for Latinx students that has allowed me to further delve into these issues.

Of course none of this would have been possible without the love and support of my family. I was so blessed to have Sonia and Milton Flores as parents. My mother's strong pride in being Puerto Rican has encouraged me to be unapologetically myself wherever I go. My father's deep passion for learning despite little formal education was the first example in my life of the vast brilliance that goes unrecognized in Latinx communities. My sister Sonia Thornton who has been a lifelong educator has been a constant reminder to me of the importance of continuing to advocate for marginalized children in spite of all of the obstacles we confront. I have also been so fortunate to have a husband like Luis Ramirez. So many years ago when I first considered entering a doctoral program I expressed doubts because of our financial situation. They immediately told me to do it and insisted that we would figure it out. Ever since Luis has never wavered in being my biggest fan and supporter. They have always been there to celebrate my accomplishments but perhaps more importantly to support me during the challenging times. I couldn't have asked for a better life partner.

The dedication to my senior thesis read "dedicated to all of the Latino students that American schools have failed to educate. Here I begin my fight for you." While I would now encourage my past self to critically interrogate what it means to be educated and insist that American schools have failed to recognize the vast amounts of cultural and linguistic knowledge that Latinx students already bring with them into the classroom, advocating for Latinx students has continued to be the motivating force for me throughout my career. So it seems appropriate to end by recommitting fighting for them in ways that continue to push toward decolonial futures.

1
One School's Journey through the Post–Civil Rights Era

In 2012, I accepted a tenure track position at the University of Pennsylvania in my hometown of Philadelphia. In line with national trends, the district was at the time expanding dual-language education programs that had the explicit goal of developing bilingualism and biliteracy for any student whose parents wished to enroll them in the program, with the goal of having relatively equal numbers of Spanish-dominant and English-dominant students. Convinced that this shift aligned with the research that pointed to the superiority of these programs over English as a Second Language (ESL) and transitional bilingual education, I soon became involved in supporting the district in these efforts. As part of these efforts, we had parent meetings at the schools selected to implement the new dual-language programs. At Washington Elementary School,[1] a school located in a gentrifying area, a white mother asked in English for my professional opinion about her desire to raise her daughter trilingually, learning English from her, Spanish from her teacher, and Mandarin from her nanny. At Hamilton Elementary School, a school located in a high-poverty predominantly Latinx area of the city, a Puerto Rican mother shared in Spanish with me that, while she didn't know what a dual-language program was, she hoped that it would help her daughter cope with the trauma she had experienced during several months when they were homeless. These were both mothers doing what good mothers do. They were trying to ensure that their children receive a high-quality education. Yet, the vast differences in the resources that they had available to them led to stark inequalities in their options.

My graduate studies prepared me to answer the question posed by the white mother. I was able to point her to research illustrating the many benefits of multilingualism for enhancing cognitive development and cultural awareness. But my education provided me with few resources for speaking to the challenges confronting the Puerto Rican mother. In fact, none of the professionals at that meeting quite knew how to respond to her concerns.

Becoming the System. Nelson Flores, Oxford University Press. © Oxford University Press 2024.
DOI: 10.1093/oso/9780197516812.003.0001

As a team, we pointed her to the school guidance counselor, as well as some local community agencies that might be able to help her. But this felt completely inadequate to the challenges facing her and her daughter—challenges that were a consequence of multigenerational poverty produced through racist public policies. The credentials that have legitimized my place within elite academic spaces provided me with few tools to address the root cause of the marginalization of this Puerto Rican mother and the many Latinx people left behind in low-income segregated neighborhoods.

This is the major issue that I will be grappling with in this book—namely, the limited impact of the rise of a Latinx professional class in the post–Civil Rights era on the lives of the majority of Latinxs living in the United States. Using bilingual education as a point of entry, I seek to critically interrogate the ways that efforts of Latinx professionals working to *transform* the system in ways that promote equity in reality led them/us to *become* the system as they/we were gradually molded into agents of institutions that have the primary function of maintaining the racial status quo. This analysis is in no way meant to diminish the important advocacy work that has led to the emergence of a Latinx professional class. Indeed, my professional successes have been made possible in large part through the tireless advocacy work of previous generations of Latinxs and their allies, and I acknowledge my deep debt to them. It is also not meant to somehow absolve me of complicity in the processes that I am critiquing here. On the contrary, it has been the discomfort with my own complicity in these processes that has motivated me to write this book. Instead, I hope to offer a critical reflection on past efforts to improve the lives of Latinxs and other racialized communities in the hopes of informing how we work to advocate for racial justice in the present and future more effectively.

In this chapter, I use the case study of the rise and fall of bilingual education at Potter-Thomas Elementary School in Philadelphia to examine the institutional context within which bilingual education emerged as a viable political strategy for serving the growing Latinx population in the 1960s, and the ways that this initial framing was part of the ideological foundation of a broader reconfiguration of race that rose to ascendency within the post–Civil Rights era. I examine the emergence of bilingual education within a broader move toward compensatory education in the 1960s. I then examine the ways that educators at Potter-Thomas sought to challenge this compensatory approach through efforts at maintaining, rather than remediating, Puerto Rican culture at Potter-Thomas. I point to the ways that, while this was framed as oppositional to the more dominant deficit framing, it relied on the same underlying logic that framed language as the primary challenge confronting the Puerto Rican community in Philadelphia, obscuring the broader structural barriers confronting this community within the context of deindustrialization. Finally, I examine the ways that Potter-Thomas was a pioneer in what would become the modern accountability movement and the ways that this would lead to its eventual demise.

Colonialism, Anti-Blackness, and Bilingual Education in Philadelphia

The rise of bilingual education in the School District of Philadelphia was shaped by massive migration to the city from Puerto Rico as a result of Operation Bootstrap, a US-supported economic reform that displaced many small farmers who were forced to seek work on the US mainland for economic survival. While most Puerto Ricans migrated to New York City, a sizable number found their way to Philadelphia. This migration began in the 1940s when groups of Puerto Rican agricultural workers who came to work in the surrounding rural areas in New Jersey began to settle in Philadelphia at the end of their contracts in search of employment in factories in the city.[2] This migration began just as the deindustrialization of the city was beginning, meaning that Puerto Ricans were coming for jobs that were disappearing. This deindustrialization, coupled with racist housing policies and white flight from Philadelphia, led Puerto Ricans to become primarily concentrated in an increasingly impoverished and segregated section of North Philadelphia with dwindling economic opportunities.[3]

The district's initial approach to supporting Puerto Rican students was to place them in "Special English classes" that had historically supported immigrant communities arriving to city schools. Jerry Miller, the director of special education, described the objective of these classes as being "to give these youngsters enough English to get them into some grade," noting that "we want to assimilate the child as quickly as possible so he can rejoin his peer group."[4] Yet, Warren Perry, the assistant director of special education, argued that there was something uniquely deficient about Puerto Rican children that made this approach less effective for them than for previous newcomers to the city, noting that it took other students "nine months to a year" to learn English, whereas it took Puerto Ricans "18 months to two years," a difference that he attributed to the fact that "they live in their little ghetto and go back there every day" and "don't try as hard as the others."[5] This perceived uniqueness of Puerto Ricans as compared to other bilingual communities situated their needs in relation to the large and growing African American population in the city, which was also framed by educators as having unique "cultural deprivations" that prevented traditional educational approaches from being effective.[6]

Efforts to connect the educational needs of African Americans and Puerto Ricans in the School District of Philadelphia coalesced in the Great Cities School Improvement Program, funded by the Ford Foundation from 1960 to 1964. This project was the outgrowth of the Great Cities Research Council, which came into being in response to the finding that whereas one of ten children in the fourteen major school districts involved in the Council were classified as "slow learners" in the 1940s, one of three children were classified as "slow learners" in the 1960s.[7] This finding, coupled with shifting perspectives in educational research away from the conceptualization of intelligence as genetic, led to the assumption that the great majority of these students were "underachievers" because of "cultural disadvantages" that led them to come "to school lacking the experiential and language supports necessary to successful achievement."[8] With this perspective at its ideological foundation, the Great Cities School Improvement Program selected seven schools in North Philadelphia with large African American and growing Puerto Rican student populations to implement "compensatory education" that entailed "a highly structured educational program, intensive in-service education of teachers, and specifically developed instructional materials."[9]

In line with the mainstream social science research that argued that "disadvantaged children" lacked verbal stimulation in their homes that prevented their academic success,[10] language was a key component in this compensatory education for the African American and Puerto Rican students being served. This was based on the assumption that "lag in language development is universally considered a critical factor in the lack of academic achievement of the disadvantaged child."[11] In response to these assumptions, the project hired a language arts consultant to work across the six schools, as well as a language arts master teacher in each school to directly coach language arts teachers on the implementation of a newly adopted and highly structured language arts program. In addition, were specific accommodations made toward incorporating Spanish into the project to support Puerto Rican students and families. This included hiring a bilingual school-community coordinator, who was charged with being the direct liaison to the Puerto Rican community and would serve as an interpreter for parental workshops and support the incorporation of culturally relevant materials into the school curriculum through organizing "a Spanish fiesta and other activities of Pan American union."[12] In addition, two schools participating in the project also hired Puerto Rican exchange teachers to develop and implement bilingual instructional approaches for Puerto Rican children and Spanish enrichment classes for the rest of the student population.[13] A similar approach to incorporating bilingual instruction was adopted by the Potter and Thomas schools as they were beginning to prepare for their eventual merger into one school that would be renamed Potter-Thomas.[14]

Funding Linguistic and Cultural Maintenance at Potter-Thomas

On November 17, 1967, Eleanor Sandstrom, a curriculum specialist in foreign languages in the School District of Philadelphia, was invited to participated in a seminar on "Puerto Rican problems" hosted by the Nationalities Service Center, a local community organization focused on advocating for "foreign born" populations in the greater Philadelphia area. While Puerto Ricans were not traditionally "foreign born" in that they were US citizens, their exponential growth in the city since the 1950s, coupled with the cultural and linguistic barriers that they confronted, put them at the top of the agenda of the Nationalities Service Center.[15] Sandstrom took this opportunity to announce that the School District of Philadelphia was moving away from Special English classes by adopting a "revolutionary educational program" that entailed "using bilingual teachers to reach Spanish-speaking children." She described this move as having "started a new kind of current in the Philadelphia school system," noting that "everybody is talking about bilingual education."[16]

It was not just in Philadelphia that everybody was talking about bilingual education in 1967. It was, rather, a national conversation that was emerging within debates about how best to meet the needs of the growing Spanish-speaking population in US schools. The emerging consensus within mainstream social science research that multiple generations of poverty had produced unique cultural and linguistic deficiencies within Spanish-speaking communities that bilingual education was well-positioned to remediate was a significant component of this national conversation, in the same ways that it had been within the Great Schools Improvement Project in the School District of Philadelphia.[17] However, within the predominantly Mexican American community in the American Southwest[18] and the predominantly Puerto Rican community in the Northeast Corridor[19] there were increasing demands for bilingual education as a way of maintaining, rather than fixing, the cultural and linguistic practices of Latinx communities within the context of the Civil Rights movement. This dynamic also played out in the School District of Philadelphia with growing demands within the Puerto Rican community for bilingual education programs that built on the cultural and linguistic practices of Puerto Rican children.[20] These community leaders worked in conjunction with district officials like Sandstrom who were increasingly critical of Special English Classes, with Sandstrom insisting that "we must preserve the culture of the ethnic community and not stamp it out."[21] While this call for cultural and linguistic maintenance seemed to be in ideological tension with mainstream social science researchers, both sides agreed that language was important to consider in the education of Latinx students, either because of their supposed verbal deprivation or because of the negative effects of schooling practices that stripped them of their home language practices.[22] This culminated in the passage of the Bilingual Education Act (BEA) in 1968, which provided federal funding to support the development of bilingual education programs to support Latinx students as well as students coming from other bilingual communities.

Sandstrom led the School District of Philadelphia in a successful application for one of the first federal grants awarded under the BEA, called the "Let's Be Amigos Program." The Let's Be Amigos program consisted of two major components. One component was the Arriba program that, building on the work that had emerged as part of the Great Cities Schools Improvement Program, sought to further develop bilingual programs in upper levels of elementary schools and high schools serving large numbers of Puerto Rican students. The second component was the Potter-Thomas Model School program that sought to develop a whole-school bilingual model. The Potter-Thomas Model School's three major aims were "to educate both native English-speaking and native Spanish-speaking students in the use of both languages, to introduce subject matter in the mother tongue (in curricular areas other than language), with selected follow-up in the second language, [and] to create a bicultural environment incorporating aspects of the Puerto Rican and mainland traditions."[23] To meet these aims, the school was divided into an Anglo strand and a Latino strand; students in each strand received 90% of their instruction in their primary language in kindergarten, with the goal being for the percentage to shift to 50% for all students by the end of elementary school. The rationale for this approach was that students "begin their cognitive development in their mother tongue [while] they begin to develop competency in listening to, speaking in, and understanding their second language."[24] In this way, the Potter-Thomas Model School sought to maintain the cultural and linguistic practices of its Puerto Rican students while also offering all the other students in the school the opportunity for bilingual development. Significantly, their intervention also sought to challenge the similar remedial framing of educational interventions for African American students by insisting that bilingual education would also be beneficial to them as well. Yet, as will be examined in the next section, the increasing segregation and poverty of the school would make these aspirations increasingly difficult to implement.

Cultural and Linguistic Maintenance within a Context of Increasing Segregation

At the time of its opening, Potter-Thomas was racially and ethnically diverse, with 42% of the students being Latinx (almost all of them Puerto Rican), 31% African American, and 27% white.[25] Yet, over the years the school became increasingly Latinx and low-income. The increase in Latinx students began when excitement about the program led to a mass influx of Puerto Rican families into the catchment area of Potter-Thomas from the time the school was announced in 1968 to when it opened the following year. This led to massive overcrowding in the first year of the program with approximately 1,500 students entering a building planned for 975 students.[26] Overcrowding would continue to plague the school while the surrounding neighborhood gradually becoming increasingly segregated as white families moved out while Puerto Rican families continued to move in.[27] By the 1980s, the neighborhood surrounding Potter-Thomas had experienced significant economic decline because of limited private-sector investment that was associated with the increasing segregation of the neighborhood, few job opportunities because of continued deindustrialization, and decreasing social supports because of the shrinking tax base of the city caused by increasing white flight.[28]

In response to the increasing segregation and poverty of the neighborhood, efforts were made to diversify the student population. One prominent example of this was the use of a BEA grant to convert Potter-Thomas into a magnet program that would accept students from outside of its catchment area as part of the school district's voluntary desegregation plan. The magnet program was described as offering "individualized instruction, provided through the use of a variety of instructional equipment located in a Bilingual-bicultural Learning Center and through small group instruction" with the goal being to "attract White, 'majority group,' pupils from outside the regular school boundaries and improve academic performance of children for whom Potter-Thomas is the neighborhood school."[29] While the school did successfully implement the learning center, it did not increase the white student population, with students attending the school from outside of the catchment area "all minority group members," most of whom "had previously attended the school."[30] Other grants would be applied for throughout the years to attract white families to the school, but the increasing segregation and poverty of North Philadelphia made this a difficult prospect. By 1997, the student body was 81% Latinx (most of whom continued to be Puerto Rican) and 18% African American, with most of the students living in deep poverty.[31]

In addition to the increasing segregation and poverty of the school was the high mobility of the student population due to continued migration to and from Puerto Rico, housing instability, and other challenges that confront high-poverty families. In a 1988 interview, William Zinn, the English reading specialist who described himself as having been an initial proponent of the bilingual program when the school began, expressed concerns about its effectiveness because of this high student mobility. He described a study that they had done ten years prior that found that only 15% of the students had been at the school from kindergarten through sixth grade.[32] In line with this, School District of Philadelphia records showed 198 admits and 235 dismissals for Potter-Thomas in the 1986–1987 school year.[33] Many of these admits were newly arrived students from Puerto Rico who would need extra English-language development support, whereas many of the dismissals indicated that students left before completing the full bilingual and biliteracy sequence of the program. Based on these findings, William Zinn asked, "So how can they reach their goals for having kids fully, more or less, bilingual in sixth grade?"[34] The challenges of student mobility would continue to confront the school into the 1990s, continuing to impact student academic performance on state standardized assessments. For example, Lorie Rosa, a fourth grader at the school, had attended kindergarten in Philadelphia, first grade in Puerto Rico, arrived back to Philadelphia in second grade, and was going to return with her parents to Puerto Rico in December of fourth grade. This was a common phenomenon as economic precarity often entailed families moving for jobs or much needed family support.[35]

The changing demographics and high student mobility also led to programmatic changes for the Anglo strand, which became increasingly African American and second- and third-generation Puerto Rican students.[36] Echoing the earlier approach to compensatory education initiated with the Great Cities Schools Improvement Plan was the assumption that many African American students entered the school with deficiencies in English and would benefit from focusing on addressing these deficiencies over learning a second language.[37] Also echoing these earlier approaches was the continued assumption that second- and third-generation Puerto Rican students would benefit from some Spanish educational intervention, though this was often discussed in relation to cultural and linguistic maintenance as opposed to deficiency (as it was discussed for African Americans).[38] Eventually, this ethnoracial distinction disappeared with a shift toward a reliance on standardized assessment data with students in the Anglo strand only provided with Spanish classes once they achieved a third-grade reading level in English.[39] That is, as the school became more segregated, it moved away from a whole-school bilingual model toward a maintenance bilingual model for Spanish-dominant students and bilingual enrichment only for English-dominant students with sufficiently high standardized test scores. Ironically, it was also at this moment of retreat from a whole-school model that the school had finally been able to successfully hire an almost completely bilingual teaching staff, with 75% of them being Latinx.[40] It was also at this time that the modern accountability movement that Potter-Thomas had been a pioneer in producing had ascended as the primary focus of educational reform.

Standardizing, Privatizing, and Ending Bilingual Education at Potter-Thomas

In 1973, Robert Offenberg, a research associate at the School District of Philadelphia Office of Research and Evaluation overseeing the internal evaluation of the BEA grant that was being used to fund the Potter-Thomas model program, received a phone call from the project director from the Office of Education. The project director was preparing to give congressional testimony and was inquiring about whether Offenberg could provide "*concrete* data showing gains or growth brought about by the project." Offenberg responded by offering data that illustrated that "the pupils could master most of the skills that project planners claimed they could." The project director insisted that "Congress did not care about meetings of expectancies—they wanted a number—an amount of gain—which they could use to show that bilingual education was 'better' than the education which it replaced."[41] This pressure would lead the school to gradually move away from teacher-made assessments based on locally developed goals toward standardized assessments designed to evaluate goals identified as relevant to the Office of Education.[42]

While Potter-Thomas would lose BEA funds in 1976, it would continue to further develop its systematic use of standardized assessment data to inform instruction. In a 1988 interview, Felicita Melendez, the principal of the school, argued that these standardized assessments were essential for the appropriate placement of students, noting that "when we get new children here, they're never placed haphazard," adding that "we have to find out what the level is, what is the language proficiency that they have, where would they fit best," concluding that "otherwise you have a mess."[43] In a different 1988 interview, William Zinn, the English reading specialist, also described the systematic tracking of student data across time and the system he had developed to track who had achieved and failed various benchmarks. As he described it, "The idea is to give them [the teachers] feedback, hey, how is the kid having trouble? And they can look deeper and see whether the kid is having trouble with word meaning, comprehension, and get more specific."[44] He proudly insisted that "I think we test more than any other school in the district" and that "it's not like this in every school," with the research interviewers also noting "we're very impressed."[45]

Potter-Thomas's increasing reliance on standardized assessments that began in response to the federal accountability system associated with the BEA offered a prelude to the federal accountability system that would emerge as part of contemporary standards-based reform. Precursors to this federal accountability system can be seen in the district's own efforts to use city-wide standardized assessments as way of beginning to rank schools. Potter-Thomas's initial performance on these assessments painted a complicated picture. On the one hand, the school consistently performed lower than most district schools. In 1975, only 26% of Potter-Thomas students scored above the 50th percentile on the California Achievement Test, ranking it 15 out of the 24 elementary schools in District 5 where it was located.[46] Yet, in defense of the school, Eleanor Sandstrom insisted that reading, math, and language skills test scores were much higher than schools in District 5 serving a similar student population.[47] In addition, scores would improve over the next few years, with 43% of the students scoring above the 50th percentile in 1979, making it one of the top 25 improved schools in the district.[48]

This dynamic continued into the 1980s and 1990s, with Potter-Thomas continuing to be simultaneously celebrated as a national model for bilingual education while also identified as a chronically underperforming school, caveats notwithstanding. For example, as it celebrated its 25th anniversary, it was described as a "model for the future" that had successfully increased the number of students reading at or above grade level from 18% to 32% in the previous four years. At the same time, it continued to rank among the lowest schools in the district, with only 10% of students scoring above the national average.[49] Based on this continued low performance, Potter-Thomas was identified as one of the district's 18 most academically troubled schools in 1995, making it a candidate to become a Quest School, which was a school redesign model developed by the district in collaboration with the local teachers' union in an attempt to improve the academic performance of these schools.[50] Though ultimately not selected for this round of reform, the school continued to be considered chronically underperforming and would be identified for an even more ambitious turnaround model in a few years after the state took over the entire school district for chronic underperformance.

The first thing that the state did after taking over the School District of Philadelphia was replace Philadelphia's nine-member school board with a School Reform Commission composed of three governor-appointed members and two mayoral-appointed members. The newly created School Reform Commission adopted a "diverse provider" model that turned over the management of the district's lowest-performing elementary and middle schools to for-profit and nonprofit organizations that were given additional per-pupil funds to lead school turnarounds in what was described as "the site of the nation's largest experiment in the private management of public schools."[51] These privatization efforts were informed by the increasingly popular educational reform that "diagnoses urban school failure as the result of lack of sound management practices by district and school leaders, union contracts that impose narrow work restrictions, and a rigid professional bureaucracy that eschews innovative practice" that should be addressed by the development of "flexible, competitive school marketplaces in which districts manage a varied portfolio of schools, providers have wide rein to innovate, and both are held accountable for student outcomes by strong contracts and through the availability of meaningful choices for students and parents."[52] Potter-Thomas was selected as one of the schools that would be handed over to a private management company and was awarded, along with 20 other schools, to Edison Schools, a for-profit company that was at the time the largest Educational Management Organization in the country, managing 100 schools nationwide.[53]

The Edison Model promised to provide a "world-class education" to all students. It sought to do this through the adoption of Success for All, a highly scripted reading program developed at Johns Hopkins University, and Everyday Math, an inquiry-based program developed at the University of Chicago. While the two programs were mandated, the decision of whether to implement a bilingual program was left to the schools with the Edison model "open to local variation."[54] Since both curricular programs were available in Spanish,[55] this made it possible for schools with bilingual programs to maintain their programs while also following the Edison Model. The Edison Model also promised to supplement this core curriculum with social studies, science, music, art, and world language, including Spanish instruction for two days in kindergarten, expanding to daily by middle school. In addition to these curricular innovations, a key aspect of the Edison Model was the Edison Benchmark system, monthly computer-based assessments in reading and mathematics designed to provide immediate results that teachers could use to identify student needs and adjust instruction accordingly.[56]

One of the first things that Edison did as manager of Potter-Thomas was to update the computer lab and develop a networked infrastructure for implementing their Benchmark testing. The Benchmark testing, which an Edison regional technical director called "a revolution," was described as allowing "teachers to get instant feedback on what students are learning and what they are missing," which can allow teachers to "tailor their lessons to the weak spots of an individual far sooner than they typically can now."[57] Yet, it wasn't actually a revolution at Potter-Thomas, which had been tracking student data in this way, albeit with less technological sophistication, since the 1980s. Just as has been the case with these previous efforts at data-driven instruction, despite the implementation of Benchmark testing, state test scores continued to lag; Potter-Thomas was identified as a Targeted School in 2007 as part of the district's Breaking the Cycle of School Failure initiative because it had failed to reach math and reading performance goals under the federal *No Child Left Behind* law for five or more years.[58] Once again failing to meet its performance goals in 2008, the School Reform Commission voted to bring Potter-Thomas back under district management.[59]

Once again under district management, Potter-Thomas was eventually selected to become a Promise Academy. As a Promise Academy, it was expected to "employ a highly structured academic program using the District's Core Curriculum and research-based reading and math interventions [and] include an English Language Learners program to accelerate the academic growth of the ELL population, as well as Transitional Bilingual and/or ESOL programs."[60] It was in the first year of implementation of the Promise Academy model that the principal decided to eliminate the transitional bilingual education program with little pushback. The same year that the bilingual program was eliminated, the school also received a new library as part of the Target School Library Makeovers program that replaced "Potter-Thomas' collection, which was 10 years old; many of its books were only in Spanish."[61] What was once seen as a revolutionary approach—in this case the presence of Spanish-language materials—was now seen as an oddity of a distant past that needed to be eliminated in the name of accountability.

Contextualizing the Rise and Fall of Bilingual Education at Potter-Thomas

Traditional narratives about the rise and fall of bilingual education at Potter-Thomas might tell the story as one related to the waxing and waning of bilingual education in the United States as the momentum of the Civil Rights movement was eventually stopped by a conservative backlash that began with the election of Ronald Regan and culminated in the banning of bilingual education in several states.[62] This is certainly an important aspect of the demise of bilingual education in Potter-Thomas, with the national backlash making the bilingual program at Potter-Thomas more vulnerable to political attack and less of a priority for the school district.[63] But this is only part of the story. At the core of the story that this chapter tells are the fundamental flaws in framing language as the primary vehicle in addressing racial inequities. In this book, I examine the ways that this focus on modifying individual behaviors, rather than addressing structural barriers, is a continuation of a broader history of colonialism that has shaped US institutions that was reconfigured to accommodate the demands of the Civil Rights movement in ways that maintained the racial status quo. To this effect, I will conduct a *raciolinguistic genealogy* that situates the institutionalization of bilingual education in the post–Civil Rights era within this broader history.

2
Raciolinguistic Genealogy as Method

In this book I conduct a *raciolinguistic genealogy* of bilingual education that situates its institutionalization in the United States in the post–Civil Rights era within broader histories of colonialism that provided its discursive foundation. A raciolinguistic genealogy has three defining characteristics. The first is a *genealogical stance* that seeks to denaturalize contemporary racial discourses by identifying the colonial relations of power that have historically made and continue to make their production possible. The second is a *materialist framing* that connects the emergence of racializing discourses to the political and economic relations of power that they were created to justify and maintain. The third is a *raciolinguistic perspective* that brings attention to the integral role of language ideologies in the racialization processes that produced and continue to maintain racial inequities.

A Genealogical Stance

Michel Foucault described a genealogical stance as premised on the idea that "humanity does not gradually progress from combat to combat until it arrives at universal reciprocity, where the rule of law finally replaces warfare; humanity installs each of its violences in a system of rules and thus proceeds from domination to domination."[1] A genealogical stance is, therefore, not focused on developing a chronology of a particular historical period. Instead, its primary focus is on examining the *grid of intelligibility* that produces normative *subject positions*, or ways of being in the world, to which all are expected to aspire.[2] It is also focused on tracing the continuities and discontinuities within the *discursive formations* that lie at the core of this grid of intelligibility across different socio-historical contexts. A genealogical stance is not as interested in taking sides in contemporary debates as it is in calling into question their very framing by exposing the power relations that have produced the contemporary grid of intelligibility that shapes them.

Becoming the System. Nelson Flores, Oxford University Press. © Oxford University Press 2024.
DOI: 10.1093/oso/9780197516812.003.0002

A genealogical perspective on race is one that examines the *politics of being* "waged over what is to be the descriptive statement of the human"[3]—that is, the onto-epistemological battle of sorting the world's population into those deemed fully human and those deemed less than fully human. Sylvia Wynter traces the emergence of modern race to the secularization of European society that led to a discursive shift away from the conceptualization of Europeans as religious subjects of the Christian church toward political subjects of the secular state, coupled with the white settler colonial conquest of what would become the Americas and the trans-Atlantic slave trade that was used to fuel the economy of these white settler colonies. She refers to the emergence of this new political subject as "Man1" and examines the ways that its discursive construction marked "the West's reinvention of its True Christian Self in the transumed terms of the Rational Self," discursively positioning "the militarily expropriated New World territories . . . as well as the enslaved Black Africa" in "the matrix slot of Otherness—to be made into the physical referent of the idea of the irrational/subrational Human Other."[4] These emerging racial logics framed Indigenous and Black populations as irrational Others, with Indigenous populations framed as incompatible with modernity and in need of elimination through genocide or forced assimilation, and Black populations as well-suited for the manual labor necessary for modernization and in need of population growth under tightly regulated conditions.[5]

The rise of the human sciences and the resulting biologization of the body led to the emergence of *biopolitics*, which Foucault defines as "the acquisition of power over man insofar as man is a living being . . . that leads to what might be termed State control of the biological."[6] Biopolitics reframed humanity as biological beings, with the modern state bestowed with the power "to 'make' live" in the sense of optimizing the productivity of desirable populations and "to 'let' die" in the sense of eliminating undesirable populations.[7] Wynter conceptualizes this framing of the population as a biological problem as a discursive shift from "Man1" to "Man2," where the matrix slot of Otherness shifted away from irrationality toward biological inferiority. Bringing particular attention to the discursive production of anti-Blackness as part of the discursive construction of Man2, Wynter argues that Blackness became "the ultimate referent of the 'racially inferior' Human other," with other colonized people framed in relation to their discursively produced proximity to Blackness (the nonhuman) and whiteness (the human).[8] That is, the discursive construction of what is conceptualized as normatively human, what Wynter refers to as the modern genre of the human, has been overrepresented as white, with this conceptualization relying on Blackness "to define its own limits and to designate humanity as an achievement"[9] and other forms of racialization discursively produced as a way of policing the borders of whiteness.[10]

In this way, a genealogical perspective goes much further than simply saying that race is a social rather than a biological construct. Instead, it examines the ways that biological views of race have become so naturalized in modern state institutions and broader societal discourses that it continues to shape the foundation of the modern grid of intelligibility even as the explicit discourse has shifted away from biological to cultural explanations for racial hierarchies. In line with this, a genealogical perspective is not interested in developing an objective racial classification system into which the world's population can be neatly sorted. Instead, its primary interest is in examining the ways that the ethnoracial categories used by the modern state to sort populations into those deemed more and less human have historically been and continue to be informed by colonial logics and have shifted across time in ways that maintain white supremacy. Below I connect this discursive approach with a materialist framing of race that brings explicit attention to the material distribution of resources that are legitimized as part of this discursive formation.

A Materialist Framing

A materialist framing connects the discursive construction of race with the inequitable distribution of resources that race was invented to justify. It starts with the premise that the rise of global capitalism would not have been possible without the exploitation and genocide of racialized communities, including through the trans-Atlantic slave trade, the white settler colonial genocide of Indigenous people, and economic imperialism.[11] A materialist view argues that changes related to global capitalism can be understood as shifts in the global political and economic world order that benefit economic elites, largely at the expense of working-class and poor people, as well as shifts in the global racial order that maintain white supremacy by subordinating and marginalizing racialized communities. More specifically, racialization processes produced as part of colonialism were integral to the rise of global capitalism, with racializing discourses used to justify the exploitation and genocide of racialized communities in service of the capitalist need for raw materials and colonized lands that they relied on enslaved labor to work. White colonizers were able to pass on the wealth that they had been able to accumulate through the exploitation and genocide of racialized communities to their children, who passed it on to their children, and so on and so forth, leading to the racial inequalities that persist today.[12]

Typical efforts to challenge racial inequalities in the contemporary world do little to address these material disparities. Instead, these interventions reify the biological hierarchies produced in the discursive construction of Man2 by presupposing an egalitarian capacity to profit from one's labor that obscures the differing structural access to capital that race was created to justify.[13] In the US context, this has often been done through focusing primarily on changing the attitudes of individuals, rather than ensuring more equitable structural access to resources.[14] From this perspective, the goal of antiracist work becomes for individuals to "see themselves as good antiracists by virtue of their antiracist feeling and desire for diversity, even as [they] continued to accrue unearned benefits from material and social arrangements that favored them."[15] In this way, modern US society can be characterized as a society of "racism without racists," with individual white people not feeling individually racist but still benefiting from the multiple generations of wealth accumulation that has provided them with access to material resources denied to racialized communities worldwide.[16] In contrast to this perspective, a materialist framing recognizes that contemporary racial inequalities are a legacy of racialized wealth accumulation and asserts that the only way to address the root cause of these contemporary inequalities is to focus on a redistribution of wealth.[17]

A Raciolinguistic Perspective

A raciolinguistic perspective connects a genealogical stance and a materialist framing of race with a focus on language ideologies in order to examine the discursive construction of *raciolinguistic ideologies* that have historically and continue to co-naturalize language and race in ways that position racialized populations as outside of what it means to be fully human.[18] Raciolinguistic ideologies were integral in producing justifications for white settler colonialism, with white settlers often depicting indigenous languages as animal-like forms of simple communication, incapable of expressing

Christian doctrine.[19] Similar raciolinguistic ideologies were used to describe the language practices of African populations both residing in Africa and in the African diaspora produced by the trans-Atlantic slave trade.[20] These raciolinguistic ideologies were part of the discursive formation of Man1 that left Black and Indigenous communities out of the dominant conceptualization of what it mean to be a fully rational human.

The Man2 shift toward a framing of racialized Others as biologically inferior produced a more Social Darwinian view of the language practices of Black, Indigenous, and other racialized communities that suggested the language practices of these communities were less evolved than European languages as a reflection of their earlier stage of human evolution.[21] This ascribed evolutionary inferiority was reflected in the management of the languages of colonized people, with the goal often being to replace colonized language practices with European ones.[22] Even in cases where European colonizers promoted the use of Indigenous languages, this was often in the service of furthering colonial domination either through efforts at instilling a sense of evolutionary inferiority in colonized subjects, or through depictions of Indigenous communities as "noble savages" whose worldviews should be protected from European influences and maintained as artifacts of human history.[23] The raciolinguistic ideologies that organized this colonial grid of intelligibility have continued to shape the world order in the postcolonial era. There are persistent traces of the argument that Indigenous communities must master European languages in order to evolve, for example, in framings of Indigenous languages as inadequate for the complex thinking processes needed to navigate the global economy.[24] In a similar vein, the need to preserve the cultural purity of "noble savages" persists in depictions of Indigenous languages in terms similar to museum artifacts that are framed as relics of earlier eras of human history.[25] Reminiscent of raciolinguistic ideologies of European colonialism, these contemporary raciolinguistic ideologies suggest that Indigenous communities must be excluded from contemporary nation-states in order to maintain their unique worldviews or must replace their Indigenous language with a European language in order to become legitimate subjects of modern states.

In short, raciolinguistic ideologies have played an integral role in constructing and maintaining racial hierarchies. In adopting a raciolinguistic perspective, I seek to denaturalize these raciolinguistic ideologies in the hopes of developing spaces of resistance that produce new discursive formations that can shape a new grid of intelligibility. Importantly, in keeping with the materialist framing adopted by a raciolinguistic genealogy, this discursive resistance must be situated within materialist struggles that seek to dismantle the white supremacist and global capitalist relations of power that raciolinguistic ideologies are part of maintaining.

A Raciolinguistic Genealogy of the United States

What follows is a brief raciolinguistic genealogy of the United States. By no means a comprehensive analysis, it is intended to provide a glimpse into the theoretical and methodological implications of a raciolinguistic genealogy for our understanding of US history. Specifically, it offers a brief overview of the ways that raciolinguistic ideologies were used to simultaneously dehumanize racialized communities while contributing to the discursive construction of whiteness that justified the material distribution of wealth in ways that privileged people discursively produced as white. It then illustrates how the demands of the Civil Rights movement were institutionalized in ways that maintain the racial status quo, which sets up the argument for the rest of the book related to the institutionalization of bilingual education.

The Dehumanizing Function of Raciolinguistic Ideologies

As was the case in other white settler colonial societies, raciolinguistic ideologies were integral components in representations of Indigenous communities by US colonizers. Specifically, Indigenous languages were depicted as products of "savage minds" that were at an earlier stage of human development than European languages and minds. These raciolinguistic ideologies were part of broader colonial efforts at dehumanizing Indigenous populations that could then be used to justify the violent conquest and genocide that white colonizers undertook against Indigenous populations throughout the United States. The consequences of this dehumanization can be found in the Declaration of Independence, which simultaneously stated that "all men are created equal" and have "the inalienable right" to "life, liberty and the pursuit of happiness" while condemning "the merciless Indian Savages." It can also be seen in the emergence of boarding schools that sought to eradicate Indigenous languages as part of efforts to "civilize" Indigenous children by forcibly removing them from their families, imposing English on them, and assimilating them into white cultural practices.[26]

Raciolinguistic ideologies were also integral components to justifying slavery and the Jim Crow laws that emerged after its abolition. For example, a British traveler to the United States claimed to not be able to understand the speech of enslaved Africans and suggested that they were "incapable of acquiring our language, and at best but very imperfectly if at all."[27] As was the case with Indigenous populations, the dehumanization that raciolinguistic ideologies played a part in producing was enshrined into the fabric of US institutions with the 3/5th compromise written into the US Constitution, which literally said that enslaved Africans were not fully human. The use of raciolinguistic ideologies would continue within the context of the Jim Crow South, where it was common for African Americans to be lynched for supposedly "speaking like a grown man or woman."[28]

Following the lead of its European predecessors, the United States also quickly became a colonial power on its own through the conquest of lands that had previously belonged to Mexico. The land that had previously belonged to Mexico was an existing white settler colonial society that, built on the discursive construction of Man1, was a state premised on the irrationality of Black and Indigenous populations.[29] The US conquest of the land created the new racialized category of "Mexican" that became mapped onto these existing racial hierarchies, alongside the move toward the discursive construction of Man2 that framed this newly constructed racialized category as biologically inferior because of their discursively constructed mixed-race heritage. While for official purposes Mexicans were classified as white—placing them closer to fully human on the grid of intelligibility than Black and Indigenous people who might also be racialized as Mexican—their claim to whiteness was "both weak and conditional" with the continued legal segregation of people racialized as Mexican from the white population a reality prior to the dawn of the Civil Rights movement.[30] Raciolinguistic ideologies were instrumental in the production of this new racialized category, with supposed language deficiencies used to justify segregating Mexican students in US schools.[31] As was the case with Indigenous children, Mexican students received corporal punishment for speaking in Spanish in the hopes of eradicating Spanish and imposing English on them.[32]

But racialized communities did not passively accept their marginalization. On the contrary, throughout US history these communities have strived to develop alternative spaces that resist their racialization. For example,

Indigenous communities created their own educational systems in response to the assimilative policies of boarding schools,[33] African Americans insisted on their right to literacy even when it was prohibited by law,[34] and Mexican Americans resisted English-Only policies by advocating for bilingual education after US colonization.[35] These acts of resistance would eventually culminate in the Civil Rights movement—a social movement that posed a fundamental challenge to the white supremacy that lies at the foundation of the United States. However, rather than dismantling white supremacy, policies developed in response to the Civil Rights movement ultimately reconfigured it in ways that ensured the maintenance of the racial status quo.

Raciolinguistic Ideologies and the Political Incorporation of the Civil Rights Movement

An oft-overlooked aspect of the Civil Rights movement was the larger sociopolitical context of worldwide revolution in which it developed. These revolutionary movements sought to instill racialized communities with a "different view of themselves and their world; different, that is, from the worldview and self-concepts offered by the established social order."[36] These efforts were eventually undermined through a process of political incorporation that "insulated the racial state from revolutionary transformation and absorbed antiracist movements in a reform-oriented transition."[37] As the demands of the Civil Rights movement became institutionalized through such measures as the Civil Rights Act, the Bilingual Education Act, and the War on Poverty, they became official forms of antiracism that "stabilized political limits, interpretive tendencies, and economic forces that readjusted and inevitably extended U.S. and transnational capitalist structures of racial domination."[38] These official forms of antiracism did little to address the multiple generations of wealth accumulation associated with whiteness as property leading to "the law's ratification of the settled expectations of relative white privilege as a legitimate and natural baseline."[39]

Ujju Aggarwal traces this focus on incremental reform to *Brown v. Board of Education*, which was the first major effort to incorporate Civil Rights demands into US institutions.[40] She analyzes the ways that the *Brown* decision shifted the burden of responsibility of social change away from the more powerful white population toward racialized communities. In particular, she points to the ways that the discourses surrounding the *Brown* decision were focused on the supposed psychological damages that African American children suffered as a result of segregation in ways that obscured the legacy of racialized material inequalities that shaped these children's lives. This can be most clearly seen in the doll test that provided the primary rationale for ending segregation. As Aggarwal documented, this test was used by Supreme Court Justice Earl Warren to suggest that segregation made Black children feel and believe that they were inferior. She documents how this discourse of psychological damage eventually was taken up in educational discourse in ways that pointed to the supposed pathologies of the African American community—rather than the structural inequalities produced through a history of white supremacy—as the primary culprit in the low academic achievement of African American students.

A court precedent that is often overlooked related to school segregation was *Mendez v. Westminster*. This decision, made in 1947 by the 9th Circuit Court of Appeals, focused on the segregation of Mexican American students in California. The argument made by Orange County school districts in defense of their segregation practices was that the segregation of Mexican American students was justifiable because of their supposed "special language needs."[41] Particularly striking in the court's decision was the primary rationale for ending this segregation, with the decision stating that "the evidence clearly shows that Spanish-speaking children are retarded in learning English by lack of exposure to its use because of segregation."[42] The decision suggested that the primary problem with the segregation of Mexican American students was not the material consequences of attending inferior schools on the generational wealth accumulation of the Mexican American community, but rather in the fact that segregation prevented them from learning English. This framing has striking similarities to the primary problem with the segregation of African American students identified by the Supreme Court in the *Brown* decision. The underlying theory of change in both decisions is that integration will fix the perceived educational deficits of Mexican and African American students, thereby ending racial inequities.

Both court precedents helped produce a discursive formation that posited that generations of poverty had produced unique cultural and linguistic deficiencies within racialized communities that prevented their social mobility.[43] Two solutions were proposed to address these cultural and linguistic deficiencies. The first one, reflected in the War on Poverty, was that the federal government should play an active role in remediating the cultural and linguistic deficits of racialized communities. The second, reflected by an emerging neoliberalism that viewed any federal intervention as amounting to handouts, was to rely on free-market mechanisms that would allow racialized communities to pull themselves up by their bootstraps. While framed as opposing political orientations, at the core of both was the basic assumption was that the legacy of racism had produced a *psychologically damaged racialized subject* who could be fixed through programs meant to instill white middle-class values and norms. In short, the reconfigured racial logic that came to prominence in the post–Civil Rights era marked a new discursive shift in Man2 that now rejected biological views of race but accepted the basic assumption of racial hierarchies with those at the bottom there because of their own cultural and linguistic deficiencies. The next chapter further explores the discursive formation of this psychologically damaged racialized subject.

3
From Community Control to Neoliberalism

In 1970, Richie Perez, a member of the Young Lords, a radical political party founded by Puerto Ricans living on the mainland, wrote an article for their newsletter calling for members of the Puerto Rican community to demand community control of schools:

> To all our brothers and sisters in school—if your school is messed up, if the administration and the teachers don't care and don't teach—don't let them force you to drop out. Throw them out. The schools belong to us, not to them. Take all that anger and put it to work for our people. Make revolution inside the school.[1]

Perez called on Puerto Rican communities to take control of their schools in order to develop community-oriented curricula that would help foster a revolutionary consciousness among Puerto Rican youth. This *race radical* vision of community control situated political struggles of the Puerto Rican community within broader efforts to promote a global revolution against global capitalism, white supremacy, and imperialism.

A year earlier, Mario Fantini, then a program officer at the Ford Foundation, a philanthropic organization that was offering a great deal of funding to educational innovation at the time, offered a somewhat different rationale for community control of schools. As he argued:

> Participation has a positive effect on the participants as well as the system. For example, as parents in East Harlem became more engaged in the education process, "quality education" replaced "Black Power" as the slogan.... The pattern of the revolutionary is that, upon assumption of power, he shifts from destroying the institutions to building order and new institutions (of his own kind, to be sure).[2]

Becoming the System. Nelson Flores, Oxford University Press. © Oxford University Press 2024.
DOI: 10.1093/oso/9780197516812.003.0003

For Fantini, putting control over these institutions into the hands of racialized communities was not revolutionary but rather counterrevolutionary, in that it undermined extremism by giving racialized communities the authority to reform existing institutions to fit their needs. In contrast to Richie Perez's race radicalism, which sought to dismantle existing institutions and create new ones, Fantini's *liberal multicultural* vision of community control sought to incorporate racialized communities into existing institutions.[3]

In 1970, Milton Friedman, a prominent University of Chicago economist, made yet another case for community control of schools in an interview with a reporter: "Community control comes through decentralization, and the only effective way to decentralize is to bring decision-making directly to the individual."[4] Friedman's vision for community control focused on individual empowerment by framing parents as consumers who were able to choose schools from a marketplace of options. This *neoliberal* vision of community control had some things in common with Perez's vision in that both desired a fundamental transformation of existing institutions. It also had some things in common with Fantini's vision in that both sought to alleviate social unrest by incorporating the voices of racialized communities into the existing institutional framework of global capitalism. Yet, at its core, Friedman's vision was fundamentally opposed to both in that these two visions focused on community empowerment, while Friedman's vision focused on individual empowerment.

Forty-five years later, I witnessed these three discursive formations in precarious alliance among school leaders at a fundraising event for a bilingual charter school in the same Philadelphia neighborhood where Potter-Thomas was located. On the one hand, the event embodied Friedman's ultimate vision. Many people at the fundraiser were members of the business community who desired a more active role in public education. As a way of convincing these prospective funders to invest in the school, the school leadership celebrated their ability to provide a high-quality educational choice for the community and had parents speak about why they chose this school for their children. Yet, traces of Fantini's discourse remained strong. This was evident in informal conversations that I had with school leaders during the event, where they emphasized the importance of bilingual education in supporting Latinx children in developing a strong sense of their cultural identity that they would be able to use to advocate for the Latinx community as future leaders within existing institutions. Less explicit but still present were discourses associated with the Young Lords. For example, a major activity was the unveiling of a mural that the students had created that included images of prominent Puerto Rican nationalists. The administrators of this school used elements from all three of these discursive formations in making the case for the importance of their school, albeit in an extremely different political climate than community-control supporters in the 1960s and 1970s could have imagined.

In this chapter, I more closely examine the grid of intelligibility that shaped the rise of community control of schools in the 1960s and 1970s, paying particular attention to the race radical and liberal multicultural support for this educational innovation. I examine how, despite key differences between them, they both relied on the discursive formation of the psychologically damaged racialized subject discussed in the previous chapter. I point to the ways that reliance on this discursive formation paved the way for neoliberal educational reforms that would become hegemonic with the conservative backlash against the gains of the Civil Rights movement in the 1980s.

The Rise of Community Control

By the late 1960s, growing disenchantment with stalled efforts at desegregation, alongside the rise of the Black Power movement, led to increasing calls among Civil Rights activists for community control of schools and other public institutions in many US cities, including Chicago,[5] Philadelphia,[6] and Washington, DC.[7] Inspired by the Black Power movement, Mexican Americans in the American Southwest,[8] Puerto Ricans in the Northeast,[9] and Native Americans on reservations[10] also mobilized for community control of schools. While these efforts were developing in response to their unique community contexts, what united them was the belief that providing racialized communities with control over the schools that their children attend would fundamentally transform them and lead to improved educational and life outcomes.

These efforts to promote community control aligned well with the call for "maximum feasible participation" of poor people in the anti-poverty programs being funded through the Johnson administration's War on Poverty.[11] This call for maximum feasible participation was informed by the culture of poverty theory that posited that the cause of poverty was cultural deficiencies within impoverished communities.[12] At the core of the cultural of poverty theory was that racial inequalities were not the result of the structural forces of white supremacy and global capitalism, but rather maladaptive cultural patterns in racialized communities that could be modified "by the state-sponsored application of technocratic and scientific expertise."[13] This framing paralleled the US government's approach to the global community within the context of the Cold War, where it sought to provide aid as part of the development of a politics of liberal multiculturalism that politically incorporated racialized communities into the existing framework of liberal democracy and global capitalism.[14] The underlying epistemological orientation of this approach accepted the premises that racialized communities were not fully evolved humans and that the state could play a key role in supporting these populations in becoming fully evolved through community participation in its institutional apparatuses.

The funding provided by the federal government to promote community participation was closely aligned with the funding priorities of liberal philanthropic organizations. Most notable in the philanthropic world were the efforts of the Ford Foundation to fund innovative educational reforms throughout the United States. As with the federal government, these efforts emerged out of the culture of poverty theory. It was this framework that led the Ford Foundation to fund the Great Cities Schools Improvement Project in the School District of Philadelphia mentioned in Chapter 1, which would become the road map for the compensatory education funded as part of the federal government's War on Poverty.[15] At the core of this compensatory education was that racialized students were not biologically inferior but rather culturally deprived, with the role of schools being to remediate these students' cultural deficits. As part of their growing racial consciousness, racialized communities in the 1960s began to speak back to these cultural deficit arguments and instead pointed to schools as the primary culprit in the educational challenges confronting racialized students.[16] Some of the most prominent groups, including the Black Panthers, embraced race radicalism and situated community control within broader efforts for the self-determination of African Americans as part of a broader global struggle against white supremacy and global capitalism.[17] This race radicalism was also adopted by parallel political organizations in other racialized communities.[18] In response to these criticisms, the Ford Foundation began to support the concept of community control.

The ability of the Ford Foundation to support community control was based on shared assumptions between their liberal multicultural vision and their race radical counterparts, especially as they related to schools. One commonality between them was a strong critique of what they perceived to be the entrenched bureaucracy of the public school system. The major argument was that the increased centralization of the US public school system alienated urban district and school administrators from the communities they served, leaving them unresponsive to the increasing diversity of their classrooms.[19] This connected to a critique of the predominantly white teachers unions that were often grouped with district and school administrators as working to shield the system from community accountability.[20] These two critiques coalesced around an image of a psychologically damaged racialized subject who had been victimized by generations of racial oppression. While coming from different political orientations, there was a fine line between a psychologically damaged racialized subject who needed liberation from white supremacy and global capitalism and a psychologically damaged racialized subject who needed to be uplifted out of the culture of poverty, with the two often advocating "paternalistic visions of social control" that positioned racialized community leaders in the role of managing low-income people from racialized communities.[21] In the following, I examine the ways that these commonalities between race radicalism and liberal multiculturalism provided a foundation for the emerging neoliberalism of the time. I do this by examining influential thinkers promoting race radicalism and liberal multiculturalism and the ways that their support for community control of schools relied on discourses that would become the foundation of the emerging neoliberal multiculturalism that would rise to hegemony in the post–Civil Rights era.

Psychologizing Colonialism, Critiquing Social Dependency

One of the most prominent manifestations of race radicalism within the context of struggles for community control of school can be found in the Black Power movement. A seminal book in this movement was *Black Power: The Politics of Liberation* by Stokely Carmichael and Charles Hamilton. The race radicalism of their analysis can be found in the ways that they situated the experiences of African Americans within a broader analysis of European colonialism. They compared the experiences of African Americans with the colonialism inflicted on Africa and other parts of the Third World, arguing that all these relationships entailed white people coming into a community to exploit its resources and ensure its economic dependence on white people. They analyze the ways that this white power structure actively produced the urban ghettos where many African Americans migrating North found themselves, arguing that "barred from most housing, black people are forced to live in segregated neighborhoods and with this comes de facto segregated schooling, which means poor education, which leads in turn to ill-paying jobs."[22] They used this analysis as a point of entry for calling for the self-determination of African Americans and other racialized communities in the United States and abroad.

A major focus of their analysis was to examine the psychological effects of domination by the white power structure on the psyche of African Americans. They noted that "from the time black people were introduced into this country, their condition has fostered human indignity and the denial of respect. Born into this society today, black people begin to doubt themselves, their worth as human beings. Self-respect becomes almost impossible."[23] Making the connection to European colonialism more broadly, they argued that "[w]hite America's School of Slavery and Segregation, like the School of Colonialism, has taught the subject to hate himself and to deny his own humanity" and pointed to the ways that "white society maintains an attitude of superiority and the black community has too often succumbed to it."[24] In a discursive move that would echo later neoliberal critiques of the welfare state, Carmichael and Hamilton offered a strong indictment of social welfare agencies, which they described as "creating a system which dehumanizes the individual and perpetuates his dependency" through a paternalistic attitude that "is no different from that of many missionaries going into Africa."[25] They referred to the federal funds offered as part of the War on Poverty as "welfare colonialism" and suggested an alternative that would shift African Americans from being "mere recipients *from* the decision-making process but participants *in* it."[26] It was within this context that they proposed Black Power as a way of simultaneously challenging the white power structure and addressing the social and psychological effects of white colonization on African Americans.

At the structural level, Carmichael and Hamilton saw Black Power as offering a political strategy for consolidating power within African American communities. As they argued, "each new ethnic group in this society has found the route to social and political viability through the organization of its own institutions with which to represent its needs within the larger society."[27] They extrapolated from this claim the idea that African Americans must have control over the institutions that serve their community, thereby transforming these institutions in ways "that will, for once, make decisions in the interest of the black community."[28] In their view, in addition to consolidating political power, community control would help African Americans overcome the psychological effects of colonization by offering the African American community a chance to develop a "positive image of itself that *it* has created."[29]

It is within this context that Carmichael and Hamilton made a case for community control of schools, arguing that it would offer an opportunity to "overcome the effects of centuries in which race has been used to the detriment of the black man."[30] Specifically, they argued that "control of the ghetto schools must be taken out of the hands of 'professionals'" who, they argued, brought with them "middle-class biases, unsuitable techniques and materials."[31] In order to dismantle the white power structure of schooling, they proposed giving African American parents authority over "hiring and firing teachers, selection of teaching materials, determination of standards" and insisted that "the principals and as many teachers as possible of the ghetto schools should be black."[32] They pointed to I.S. 201, one of New York City's demonstration districts at the time experimenting with community control, as a model, arguing that the struggle at I.S. 201 was part of the consciousness-raising of the African American community that would undo the psychological damage of colonization and ultimately lead to an independent school board for the African American community. They concluded that "such an innovation would permit the parents and the schools to develop a much closer relationship and to begin attacking the problems of the ghetto in a communal, realistic way."[33]

In summary, Carmichael and Hamilton situated the experiences of African Americans within the broader system of European colonialism that marginalized racialized communities worldwide. At the core of their analysis was the image of psychologically damaged racialized subjects whom they framed as broken and in need of fixing so that they could discover their full humanity and thus be able to benefit from liberation. Their description of African Americans as overly dependent on federal funds and social welfare agencies paralleled the emerging critique associated with neoliberalism that was beginning to promote free market solutions and choice as a strategy for empowering African Americans and other racialized communities to escape this dependency.[34] As I discuss in the next section, liberal multiculturalists inspired by the Black Power movement and the emerging neoliberal discourse also began to focus on market-based reforms in response to the bureaucratic backlash that ended most experiments in community control by the early 1970s.

Dismantling Centralized Bureaucracies through Competition

One of the most prominent liberal multicultural organizations supporting community control was the Institute for Community Studies, housed at Queens College and directed by Marilyn Gittell and Maurice Berube. The Institute was funded by the Ford Foundation to support and document the work being done in three community-controlled demonstration districts in New York City.[35] There are many overlaps between the rationale for community control of schools offered by the Institute for Community Studies and by Carmichael and Hamilton. For one, the Institute directors were critical of the role that the public school bureaucracy was playing in the continued disenfranchisement of African Americans and other racialized communities, arguing that "isolated city school bureaucracies [have] shown themselves incapable of adapting to shifting educational needs."[36] Gittell connected this lack of responsiveness to a broader political project of "a small group in the centralized city school system" that was working to "maintain its position of power."[37] She identified these centralized bureaucrats' lack of responsiveness and desire to maintain political power as "ultimately responsible for the expansion of the concept of community participation to community control."[38]

In line with Carmichael and Hamilton's call for community control, the directors of the Institute for Community Studies also framed community control as working to undo the psychological damage of racism on African American and other racialized communities. Specifically, Berube relied on elements of the Black Power framework introduced by Carmichael and Hamilton to justify the focus on community control over desegregation, arguing that "black school children suffered psychological damage in segregated schools *because the prevalent values in these schools were white*."[39] He contrasted this with the vision proposed by Black Power advocates, suggesting that "in this context of a 'segregated' school system emphasizing black values, one can conceive of psychological benefit to black children."[40] Specifically, he argued that the centralized bureaucracies of urban school districts "generate feelings of powerlessness and alienation among parents and pupils."[41] In contrast, he argued that community control of schools would "strengthen pupils' feelings of control over their destinies," ensuring that students develop "a greater sense of self-worth [that] would correspondingly develop a greater motivation to learn."[42] "A feeling of control over one's destiny," he asserted, "influences achievement."[43]

Yet, instead of calling for complete self-determination for African Americans through the development of separate school systems, the Institute for Community Studies called for introducing competition within the existing public school system. Relying on discourses that would come to characterize the emerging neoliberalism of the time period, Gittell argued that expanding community control would inevitably "assure an expansion in the number of kinds of alternatives offered and a greater willingness to experiment," with the system becoming "more responsive to innovation."[44] Gittell and Berube warned that if centralized bureaucracies continued to prevent community control and its associated innovations, it could lead to "the end of public education." They specifically noted that failing to incorporate African Americans into the system would lead them to establish "alternative forms of school systems that are more attuned to their needs."[45] Gittell described a growing interest within the African American community and other racialized communities for such "alternate or parallel private school systems which are operated by the community,"[46] suggesting this as a possible approach for breaking free of the entrenched centralized bureaucracies that characterized urban public school systems.

As it became clear that the community-control experiments in New York City were going to be abolished, alongside the bulk of the community-control experiments taking place in urban school districts around the country, the Institute began to push even more forcefully for alternatives outside of public school bureaucracies. This shift can be seen in Berube's relatively supportive exploration of the Nixon administration's proposed vouchers program. Writing for the Institute newsletter, Berube described the voucher plan as embodying "one of the most significant educational ideas of our time: that every child has different learning strengths and learning paces."[47] He argued that "under the voucher plan, theoretically, parents may choose from schools employing many educational approaches."[48] and indicated that "the idea of educational alternatives constitutes the best reason for vouchers."[49] He also saw the voucher plan as being able to "cut through the infrastructure of school bureaucracies impeding reform," enabling "school professionals to break from the Oedipal mold of central school bureaucracies."[50] It was in this ability to bypass the school system bureaucracies that Berube saw the strongest parallels with community control, and it was this parallel that Berube identified as the primary reason for opposition from the teachers' union, which he defined as "defenders of the *status quo*."[51]

Berube envisioned an alliance between proponents of this voucher plan and "highly experimental approaches such as open schools . . . most of which are part of the community control movement" that would be able to overcome the resistance of teachers' unions. He noted that this alliance would ensure the survival of these schools that he characterized as living "a precarious foundation existence and . . . desperately in need of government funding."[52] While he was concerned that the voucher plan would not "heighten the self-esteem" of African American parents and would instead convert them into the relatively passive role of consumers who could "only vote with their feet,"[53] he concluded that "the voucher plan could create exciting options to public education."[54]

In short, while Carmichael and Hamilton identified colonial relations of power as the primary root of racial inequalities, Gittell and Berube identified the centralized bureaucracies of schools and other public institutions as the primary culprit. Despite these differences in their point of entry, both pairs saw community control as a viable option for beginning to address these racial inequalities by helping to alleviate the psychological damage that had served to dehumanize the African American population across the United States. While Carmichael and Hamilton saw community control as a first step toward the complete self-determination of the African American community and the liberation of racialized communities worldwide, Gittell and Berube saw it as a way of introducing more competition into the system by bringing parent and community perspectives to the table to compete with professional perspectives of teachers and administrators in order to develop new educational innovations. With community-control efforts facing strident opposition from these education professionals, Gittell and Berube began to promote the creation of alternative schools and alternative school systems that would be developed by African American and other racialized communities to compete with existing schools and school systems. As with the critique of the welfare state posed by Carmichael and Hamilton, this call for more competition aligned well with the emerging neoliberalism of the time period.

Toward a Raciolinguistic Perspective on Community Control

This book seeks to add a raciolinguistic perspective to community-control struggles, with a particular focus on struggles for bilingual education that emerged in tandem with struggles for community control. Notably, it was within the context of the Ocean Hill–Brownsville experiment in community control in New York City that Luis Fuentes, the first appointed Puerto Rican principal in the city, developed a bilingual education program to serve the sizable Puerto Rican population residing in the community.[55] As part of these efforts, African American students in the district were also offered the opportunity to learn Spanish. In addition, Swahili was offered as part of the Africanist push of the curriculum that was undertaken under the direction of the local governing board.[56] These examples illustrate that issues of language in general, and bilingual education in particular, were seen as essential tools in dismantling the white power structure of mainstream schooling and in empowering students and parents within the community. A central role of language in the fight for community control within racialized communities can also be seen in the advocacy for bilingual education among Mexican American activists[57] in the American Southwest and among Native American activists residing on reservations.[58]

Yet, as biological explanations of racial disparities shifted to cultural explanations, language also became a key mechanism for justifying the continued maintenance of racial inequities. Traces of this can already be seen in the cultural and linguistic deficit frameworks utilized by programs and organizations funded by the federal government and the Ford Foundation in the 1960s. They can even be seen in the supposed educational innovations emerging from experiments in community control. One such educational innovation that emerged in Ocean Hill–Brownsville was the Bereiter-Engelmann method.[59] This method was informed by the verbal deprivation theory that posited that low-income children from racialized backgrounds lacked appropriate verbal stimulation at home and, therefore, needed intensive remediation when they arrived in school.[60] The method and assumptions behind it were vehemently critiqued by scholars within the emerging field of sociolinguistics who pointed to the complexity of all language varieties.[61] These sociolinguists, along with educators like Eleanor Sandstrom, mentioned in Chapter 1, began to advocate for pedagogical approaches that built on the linguistic and cultural knowledge of racialized students, as opposed to framing them as deficient and in need of remediation. One such approach favored by sociolinguists and educators who adopted this perspective was bilingual education;[62] that is, bilingual education was framed as an anti-racist alternative to the Bereiter-Engelmann method and other deficit perspectives.

In the rest of this book, I challenge this framing by pointing to the ways that the institutionalization of bilingual education relied on the same image of the psychologically damaged racialized subject, shaping struggles for community control of schools. Indeed, elements of this psychologically damaged racialized subject can be seen in the race radicalism of the Young Lords, who positioned bilingual education as combating "psychological imperialism" and opening up the opportunity for "teaching our people pride in being boriqueños, that Puerto Rican Spanish is not a bastard knowledge, and that we should all attempt to learn it."[63] A similar psychological framing can be found in the rationale for bilingual education within Ocean Hill–Brownsville offered by Luis Fuentes, when he argued that "the first thing blacks lost when they were brought as slaves to America was their language. When you lose your language you lose identity."[64] This discourse not only reproduced the psychologically damaged racialized subject, but also suggested that African Americans were even more fundamentally damaged than the Puerto Rican students being served by the bilingual program who might still be able to maintain their identity. In this way, bilingual education, like many other policies institutionalized in response to demands of the Civil Rights movement, has primarily served as a tool of social reproduction, as opposed to social transformation in the ways that many of its supporters have hoped.

4

The Bilingual Revolution Will Not Be Funded

In July 1969, the Board of the recently created Southwest Council of La Raza (SWCLR) had a meeting about whether to change their priorities. In their one year of operation they had primarily supported local grassroots struggles focused on improving the lives of Mexican Americans, with one of their primary focuses being to support struggles for bilingual education. Yet, supporting these grassroot political struggles had often put them into conflict with the Ford Foundation, which was their primary funder. The Ford Foundation had recently come under fire by both conservatives and liberals for funding organizations accused of engaging in militant political actions to promote radical social change. It had decided, in response to these criticisms, to shift its monetary support toward less politically contentious projects.[1] As a result, the Foundation was pressuring the SWCLR to move away from supporting grassroots political struggles toward the adoption of a top-down programmatic model with clear deliverables. The meeting was tense and became heated as Board members debated whether to comply with the Foundation's request or risk losing their funding. Henry Santiestevan, one of the board members later reported:

> Maclovio [Barraza] and I led the battle to go programmatic, and we won. Bert Corona was on the other side. He wanted to stay militant and activist and to hell with everybody. And you know, way down deep in our guts, we were sympathetic. But we also knew it could ruin us.[2]

The Board, therefore, reluctantly agreed to the request, leading Bert Corona and other more radical members of the Board to resign. Their resignation, alongside a $1.3 million grant from the Ford Foundation, led the organization to rebrand itself as a professional advocacy organization known as the National Council of La Raza (NCLR), far removed from its grassroots origins.[3] This shift was applauded by a Foundation report as a "programmatic

Becoming the System. Nelson Flores, Oxford University Press. © Oxford University Press 2024.
DOI: 10.1093/oso/9780197516812.003.0004

shift in emphasis from direct support for barrio organizations in the Southwest to the role of advisor and spokesman for the Mexican-American community."[4]

While race radicalism may have accepted the psychologically damaged racialized subject that lay at the core of dominant approaches to explaining racial inequities, its focus on fighting for large-scale social transformation through grassroots political struggle still proved too dangerous for philanthropic organizations seeking to address racial inequities, leading these organizations to use the power of the purse to pressure these organizations to move toward professionalized forms of advocacy work in line with liberal multiculturalism.[5] In the case of the Latinx community, the Ford Foundation supported these efforts through funding the creation of professional organizations,[6] supporting the creation of ethnic studies programs,[7] and supporting bilingual education and other educational innovations that promised to improve educational outcomes for Latinx students.[8] In this chapter, I explore the ways that these efforts worked to reframe debates pertaining to bilingual education through the strategic mobilization of resources in ways that sought to minimize political controversy and by molding Latinx community activists into professionals who were able to attain more proximity to whiteness by accepting that the root of the problem lay in their community's cultural and linguistic deficiencies and the solution being to fix these deficiencies.

The Ford Foundation's Path to Bilingual Education

At the dawn of the Civil Rights movement, language education was already an interest of the Ford Foundation. In particular, the Foundation positioned English-language development as a necessary component of the modernization of emerging postcolonial nations.[9] As a result, by the mid-1960s the Foundation was funding hundreds of projects seeking to improve English-language instruction.[10] Gradually, the Foundation began to shift its focus away from a sole focus on English-language instruction toward the promotion of local and regional languages, in addition to English.[11] The Foundation situated this shift toward support for promotion of local and regional languages within broader efforts to support US interests within the international context of the Cold War under the assumption that promoting local and regional languages in postcolonial societies would create a nationalist buffer against the spread of communism and in favor of liberal democracy and capitalism.[12]

The Foundation conceptualized their support for bilingual education in the United States in similar ways, with bilingual education fitting into the Foundation's vision of improving race relations by supporting racialized communities in successfully assimilating into mainstream liberal democratic and capitalist institutions.[13] This vision intersected with Cold War politics that elevated Spanish to a politically important role with the influx of primarily middle- and upper-class Cuban refugees into the United States. Because they were seen as reluctant visitors from relatively privileged backgrounds who were strategic political allies in the fight against communism, Cubans found themselves in more hospitable environments than other Latinxs such as Mexicans and Puerto Ricans.[14] The idea was that it was important for Cuban refugee children to maintain their Spanish to prepare for their return once Castro was overthrown, even as they learned English to adapt to their temporary home.[15] In line with this idea, the Ford Foundation provided support to help open Coral Way Elementary School, a bilingual school targeting both Spanish-dominant Cuban refugees and English-dominant students.[16]

Whereas the Foundation's funding of Coral Way was framed within supporting political allies within the context of the Cold War, the Foundation's funding for bilingual education through its support of SWCLR stemmed from the culture of poverty theory. For example, one program officer suggested that the "major deficiencies of Mexican American communities are divisiveness and argumentiveness, low trust in their leaders, and an absence of a sense of priorities and progress," with his hope being that the SWCLR "could bring together the many disparate themes of Mexican-Americans, offer a strong voice and programs, strengthen leadership capabilities, and promote the capacity at the neighborhood and city level to conduct programs that will improve the economic position of the poorer Mexican-Americans and deepen their political participation."[17] The SWCLR's original leadership team adopted the same discursive formation as the Foundation in its proposal for funds, asserting that "economic deprivation and linguistic damage combined explain the low rate of college attainment of Mexican-American youth."[18] Yet, the organization prioritized funding grassroots community-organizing efforts that responded to the immediate needs of the local communities most impacted by existing local policies.[19] This provided space for more race radical activists to use the funding available to support militant political action against the white power brokers in local affiliates.[20]

These political actions led the Foundation to be accused of funding militant extremists and "stirring up revolutionary activities among the ordinary peaceful and patriotic Mexican Americans in our southwestern states."[21] Most contentious was the SWCLR's decision to subcontract funds to the Mexican American Youth Organization (MAYO) to improve education in San Antonio and the Southern Texas Valley. Founded by five Mexican American college students in 1967, MAYO was an organization built around the cultural nationalism of Chicanismo that offered a critique of "gringo institutions" such as schools that were seen as key instruments in the colonization of the Mexican American community. MAYO leaders combined this relatively broad ideological framework with a strong belief in the need to organize directly within the Mexican American community around the issues that were identified as most relevant to community members.[22] A key aspect of their political strategy was to directly confront white political opponents in the hopes of challenging the stereotype of Mexican American subservience and with the goal of getting their opponents to show their racism.[23] These confrontational tactics served to raise MAYO's profile and position it as a key leader in the Mexican American community.[24]

A primary component in MAYO's political agenda was to challenge what they believed to be the educational genocide occurring within San Antonio area public schools. A primary focus of this organizing work were efforts to dismantle district policies that prohibited Spanish and to promote bilingual education as an alternative. Indeed, one of their major accomplishments was successfully advocating the overturning of policies that prohibited the use of Spanish in all seventeen San Antonio school districts and the initiation of legislation to promote bilingual education, to develop bilingual curricular materials, and to test the efficacy of these programs and materials.[25] These efforts to implement educational policies that built on the cultural and linguistic knowledge of Mexican American students fit into their broader vision of dismantling gringo institutions and replacing them with community-controlled ones.[26]

MAYO leaders were initially able to strategically position themselves in ways that allowed them to indirectly receive both governmental and philanthropic funding for their political organizing work. In the case of the Ford Foundation, they were able to tap into funding provided to the SWCLR through the development of the Mexican American Unity Council (MAUC), a nonprofit educational development corporation started and led by MAYO leaders that received funding from the SWCLR to support its work within the San Antonio community. MAUC provided both full-time employment for MAYO leaders while also directly providing MAYO with $10,000 that it used to hire a staff person and engage in local community-organizing work.[27] While this funding was vital to supporting this organizing work, it also proved to be a double-edged sword, as MAYO's increasing reliance on funding began to come into conflict with MAYO's confrontational approach to community organizing.

In particular, MAYO's confrontational tactics were condemned by mainstream white and Mexican American politicians, most notably Congressman Henry González, who openly condemned MAYO on the floor of the House of Representatives. He also condemned the Ford Foundation's support for MAYO, suggesting that "the best designed of grants may well be meaningless if the grantees have no judgment, dedication, skill or energy."[28] Yet, Gonzalez was not the only person pressuring the Foundation to withdraw its support for MAYO. Complainants writing letters to the Foundation described MAYO as a "Castro type organization"[29] whose office was "plastered with Che Guevara posters"[30] and compared the group to the anti-Semitic groups that Henry Ford had been known to support in his lifetime.[31] Particular attention was brought to comments made by José Angel Gutiérrez, one of the founders of MAYO, who argued that "some Mexicanos will become psychologically castrated, others will become demagogues and gringos as well, and others will come together, resist and eliminate the gringo. We will be with the latter."[32] Complaints to the Foundation argued that Gutiérrez wanted to kill all gringos,[33] with Congressman Gonzalez suggesting that Gutiérrez's rhetoric showed that he was no different than a white segregationist.[34] Because many of the complaints were actually mailed to the Ford Motor Company as opposed to the Ford Foundation (two separate organizations with different Boards), the Foundation also found itself under pressure from the Company because of concerns that their support for supposedly militant groups was hurting the Company's bottom line.[35]

The Foundation tried to defend MAYO by celebrating its gains related to bilingual education. The Foundation also insisted that Gutiérrez's comment was taken out of context and was referring to "the elimination of the racist attitudes held by some white men so that the Mexican American could be free to fulfill his potential as a citizen with dignity and security."[36] Nevertheless, they found themselves increasingly under pressure and, in turn, placed pressure on the SWCLR to reign in MAYO and other local community groups receiving funds. MAYO's continued involvement in controversial political activities eventually led the Foundation to refuse to renew funds for the organization, with their justification being that MAYO was engaged in partisan political activities that the Foundation could not fund for fear of losing its tax exempt status.[37] It also prompted the Foundation to impose new strict rules on the SWCLR that mandated the organization to divert its efforts away from community organizing and advocacy toward the development of "hard programs" with measurable objectives that would be pre-approved by the Foundation.[38]

As the SWCLR began to adopt this new "hard program" approach, it also sought to expand its efforts beyond the American Southwest by becoming a national organization focused on advocating for Mexican Americans across the country. This led the organization's leaders to change the name to the National Council of La Raza (NCLR) and gradually shift its focus toward serving as a professional liaison to federal government agencies and corporations, primarily through the release of public statements on pending legislation and through a focus on business projects within Latinx communities.[39] These efforts began at the same time that the Bilingual Education Act (BEA) was being formalized into policy guidance for states and districts, with the NCLR shifting its efforts to compiling research related to best practices in the hopes of influencing these federal policies and the ways that they were being implemented in states and districts.[40] In this regard, despite having experienced some political backlash, funding the SWCLR and its transition to the NCLR was a resounding success from the perspective of the Foundation, as illustrated by Ford Foundation President McGeorge Bundy's comments in 1970 that the NCLR had "taken the first steps toward converting the long pent-up anger and frustration of its people, ever in danger of explosion and violence, into beneficial programming and planning," noting that the Foundation was "glad to assist in their pioneering effort to provide constructive direction to the growing energy and momentum of the Mexican-American movement."[41]

More race radical political activists condemned the increasingly top-down nature of the NCLR, with Bert Corona accusing the Council of being "beholden to the Ford Foundation" which "limited the effectiveness and autonomy of the group and steered it toward more of an establishment perspective"[42] and MAYO founder José Angel Gutiérrez arguing that reliance on Foundation funding made the NCLR "less accountable and accessible to Chicano militants, activists, and community that they purported to represent."[43] Some race radical critics sought to sustain their work outside of the NCLR and other mainstream institutions.[44] Yet, many race radical critics decided to try to effect change from within existing institutions through a focus on voter registration and electoral politics, which provided them a point of entry into these institutions that wasn't reliant on philanthropic funding.[45]

MAYO leaders adopted this second tactic. By the early 1970s, they had refocused attention away from grassroots community organizing to partisan politics through the development of La Raza Unida Party (RUP) that was designed to be a third-party alternative to the white-dominated Republican and Democratic parties.[46] One major victory of the RUP was, in the spirit of the struggle for community control of schools, successfully taking over the Crystal City School Board, where they were able to implement a range of educational reforms. Yet, having done so, they once again found themselves reliant on funding, in this case federal funding. In particular, the Board was able to use federal funds to create a K–12 bilingual education program that was celebrated as a national model.[47] Yet, political controversy resulting from Board actions, such as firing white and conservative Mexican American teachers and administrators seen as unsupportive of RUP's vision for the schools and mandating that all staff members become bilingual, coupled with the beginning of federal retrenchment away from supporting bilingual education, led to gradual decreases in funding that made the programs difficult to sustain.[48] As a result, by the 1980s, the bilingual education program had shifted away from a K–12 maintenance model to a transitional model focused exclusively on early elementary school.[49] This demise of the bilingual education program in Crystal City paralleled the decline of RUP, which, as a result of political attacks to keep it off ballots, voter suppression tactics, government surveillance and infiltration, and campaigns to discredit key leaders, had disbanded by the early 1980s, with many former RUP members becoming part of the Democratic Party.[50] One might be tempted to suggest that if only activists had stayed true to their race radical principles, the story may have ended differently. Yet, as the next case study shows, a loyal commitment to race radical principles was increasingly difficult to maintain within the context of an increased reliance on the philanthropic community in supporting racial equity work.

The Ford Foundation, Puerto Ricans, and Bilingual Education

Paralleling its support for bilingual education within Mexican American communities in the American Southwest, the Ford Foundation also supported bilingual education for the Puerto Rican community in the Northeast. Sometimes this support emerged spontaneously, as was the case of Ocean Hill–Brownsville, where the local governing board approved the creation of a bilingual education program without receiving prior approval from the Foundation.[51] Other times, the Foundation took a more active role in providing funding to support bilingual education. This active role primarily stemmed from the increasing concern among Foundation staff that their support for community control of schools primarily focused on the African American community. In the case of New York City, the idea for counteracting this tendency was to provide funds that targeted the Puerto Rican and Chinese communities to "balance its interest with minorities"[52] with a sizable amount of these funds going to support a range of bilingual education initiatives.

Aspira was one of the community organization within the Puerto Rican community that received support from the Ford Foundation.[53] In line with the Foundation's educational vision, Aspira encouraged Aspira youth, known as Aspirantes, to actively participate in public hearings, press conferences, and demonstrations in support of community control of schools.[54] This focus on community control of schools aligned with the Foundation's commitment to support the development of a cadre of leaders within racialized communities who could support these communities in successfully assimilating into mainstream society. Based on this vision, they saw an opportunity to support Aspira in its efforts to promote leadership development within the Puerto Rican community, with these leaders serving as "a broad base of competent professionals that might initiate and implement a sorely needed systematic approach to community development."[55] In line with this perspective, in 1968, the Foundation provided funding to Aspira to develop organized affiliates in Chicago, Newark, San Juan, and Philadelphia, centered on Puerto Rican leadership development through a focus on college and career access.[56]

More race radical Aspirantes perceived Aspira's approach to be too individualistic in its framing and too accommodating to the white supremacist status quo. In the case of Aspira of Pennsylvania, these critics were not content to simply learning about their cultural heritage while advancing their own career objectives, but were instead interested in focusing on challenging the impacts of white supremacy and global capitalism on the marginalization of Puerto Ricans residing in Philadelphia. In response to their frustrations, they formed the Philadelphia Branch of the Young Lords in

1970.[57] Adopting the platform and approach of the New York Young Lords, the Philadelphia branch situated calls for bilingual education within a larger struggle that sought to dismantle white supremacy and explicitly critiqued the inequities perpetuated by global capitalism and imperialism.[58] Members of the Philadelphia Young Lords sought to expose Puerto Rican youth to a radical political education that was designed to raise their consciousness as part of laying the groundwork for revolutionary social change. One way that they sought to do this was through the development of a free breakfast program for Puerto Rican students that included race radical content, such as "a lesson about why the kids' parents can't afford the food boys and girls need in order to do well in school."[59] In addition, members of the Philadelphia Young Lords sought to partner with local organizations and Philadelphia schools in order to offer presentations that sought to introduce this more race radical perspective to the broader community.[60] They also engaged in a range of direct action campaigns to raise awareness of issues affecting the Puerto Rican community in Philadelphia.[61]

Their race radical views and militant tactics made it difficult for the Philadelphia Young Lords to gain access to the communities that they were hoping to transform. As an example, the Philadelphia Young Lords had to lobby aggressively to be able to offer their free breakfast program at Lighthouse, a local nonprofit that served large numbers of Puerto Rican youth and families. The staff of Lighthouse finally agreed to allow them to use the space for their breakfast program, but would not offer any funds to support the initiative because of concerns about their radical ideology.[62] There was also a huge backlash from many of the white families participating in programming at Lighthouse, who took their complaints to the United Fund, which provided most of Lighthouse's operating budget. In response, the day after the first free breakfast began, the United Fund placed Lighthouse on probation and took away their funding.[63] While the funds were eventually restored, this was done in response to the nonprofit community condemning the United Fund's overriding the professional judgment of nonprofit staff, rather than in support of the Philadelphia Young Lords.[64] Indeed, this incident was part of a broader backlash against the Philadelphia Young Lords that served to further isolate them from the community that they sought to support, as demonstrated by the backlash that they also received after conducting a presentation for students at a local school, with district officials vowing never to allow them to participate in school functions again.[65]

In short, while the Philadelphia Young Lords held on to their race radical vision, they became increasingly marginalized within the educational scene and within mainstream political debates. This isolation, alongside extreme political repression, led both the local and national organization to recoil into theoretical debates that were far removed from the lived realities of the community that they purported to represent.[66] In 1972 the national organization changed its name to the Puerto Rican Worker's Revolutionary Organization and formally adopted a Marxist-Leninist-Maoist position that refocused its efforts away from direct action within the Puerto Rican community and toward organizing the industrial proletarian class in factories.[67] Both the national and local organization would disband by 1975. Though many former members would continue to be engaged in Philadelphia politics through various leftist organizations such as the Puerto Rican Socialist Party and the Puerto Rican Alliance, each of these organizations would suffer a similar fate to the Philadelphia Young Lords, collapsing within a few years.[68] A primary reason for the lack of sustainability for these organizations was the fact that more moderate liberal multicultural organizations, including Aspira of Pennsylvania, were working to institutionalize a vision of racial justice and bilingual education that was less threatening to the white supremacist status quo.

A primary strategy that Aspira of Pennsylvania leaders adopted to advocate for bilingual education was the judicial route, through the filing of a class action lawsuit against the School District of Philadelphia on behalf of four Puerto Rican parents for a failure to provide their children with appropriate bilingual education services. The lawsuit was based on the claim that at least 500 Spanish-dominant students were not receiving language support of any kind and that the vast majority who were receiving services were receiving ESL services, with "truly bilingual programs" existing in only nine schools.[69] Yet, even the nature of these "truly bilingual schools" was questionable, with Sister Francis, a bilingual education activist, describing one such school as having "one Hispanic teacher, a Spaniard, and about 5 ESL teachers, all Anglos," insisting that "they call the school a bilingual one and they point to the fact that the principal is Puerto Rican."[70] This claim was further corroborated by a teacher at the school in question, who reported that "ten of the 35 pupils in my home room barely speak English. I do not speak Spanish. . . . I'm not sure how many of the kids understand what we're saying."[71] The suit was dropped in 1977, when the District agreed to a nonbinding resolution indicating their support for bilingual education.[72]

Despite signing this resolution, the school district did little to improve or expand bilingual education and, in an attempt to reduce the district deficit, implemented severe cuts that resulted in the firing of ninety-one bilingual teachers in 1981.[73] By the end of the 1980s, there were only three official transitional bilingual programs remaining in the District.[74]

In short, Aspira's liberal multicultural vision of seeking court support for the institutionalization of a remedial form of bilingual education was successful at retaining the financial support of the Ford Foundation and other philanthropic organizations. Yet, this institutionalization of bilingual education represented a significant compromise of the vision of bilingual education that many Puerto Rican community activists promoted, disconnecting it from a grassroots struggle informed by race radicalism and turning it into a professionalized intervention led predominantly by Latinx experts informed by liberal multiculturalism. While one might argue that it was a necessary political compromise, it wasn't particularly effective, as demonstrated by Aspira of Pennsylvania's failed efforts to pressure the School District of Philadelphia to expand bilingual education.

The Funding Catch-22

This chapter points to a catch-22 that confronted many Latinx activists working to promote bilingual education within the context of the Civil Rights movement and its aftermath. On the one hand, philanthropic support provided necessary resources that could be used to mobilize communities in support of bilingual education and other policies that would have a meaningful impact on their lives. On the other hand, accepting this financial support came with certain strings attached that pushed activists to compromise in ways that they felt were politically necessary, if not necessarily philosophically aligned with their true vision of bilingual education. It might be tempting to condemn those who accepted funding in ways that compromised their vision and argue that if only they had maintained their convictions, the story of bilingual education in the post–Civil Rights era might have been different.

Yet, as illustrated in this chapter, simply refusing to conform to funder expectations didn't magically remove bilingual education activists from the broader philanthropic structure that was becoming increasingly important in funding Civil Rights causes. On the contrary, the philanthropic funding apparatus served to isolate those who maintained race radical commitments in ways that prevented them from making inroads into the communities they purported to be working to transform. In the end, it was funders, rather than Latinxs community leaders, who had the ultimate say over what demands for bilingual education would look like in the post–Civil Rights era. Accepting the psychologically damaged racialized subject as the root of the problem wasn't sufficient if this was situated within a broader structural analysis that posed an existential threat to liberal democracy and global capitalism, as was the case with race radicalism. What these philanthropic organizations wanted was to support liberal multicultural initiatives that provided limited proximity to whiteness for a cadre of Latinx professionals that they could use to say that they were doing something to challenge racial inequalities when, in reality, they were working to reify the racial status quo.

5

Producing Deficiency and Erasing Colonialism in the Bilingual Education Act

On January 17, 1967, Texas Senator Ralph Yarborough gave a speech on the Senate floor proposing new federal legislation in support of bilingual education. Focusing his comments primarily on Mexican Americans, he argued that "the time has come when we must do something about the poor schooling, low health standards, job discrimination, and the many other artificial barriers that stand in the way of the advancement of the Mexican-American people along the road to economic equality," noting that "the most promising area for progress is in the field of education."[1] He argued that English-only instruction led the Mexican American child to "believe from his first day of school that there is something wrong with him, because of his language," which he argued "indelibly imprints upon the consciousness of young children an attitude which they will carry with them all the days of their lives," leading to "psychological damage [that] shows up in test scores."[2] He described the proposed legislation as addressing this issue by providing federal funding for "programs designed to impart to Spanish-speaking students a knowledge of and pride in their ancestral culture and language," which he saw as "a magnificent opportunity . . . to enable naturally bilingual children to grow up speaking both good Spanish and good English, and thereby to be in a position to go forth confidently to deal with the world, rather than retreat in embarrassment from a world which speaks a language which they understand only imperfectly."[3]

Almost a year later, on January 2, 1968, Title VII of the Elementary and Secondary Education Act (ESEA), also known as the Bilingual Education Act (BEA), was signed into law by President Lyndon Johnson after passing both chambers of Congress with overwhelming bipartisan support. In this chapter, I will argue that the reason that the BEA was able to so easily pass was because it was part of a broader reconfiguration of racial logic that politically incorporated the demands of the Civil Rights movement in ways that accepted racial hierarchies as given, if now cultural rather than biological.

Becoming the System. Nelson Flores, Oxford University Press. © Oxford University Press 2024.
DOI: 10.1093/oso/9780197516812.003.0005

This shift away from biological to cultural explanations for racial hierarchies refocused attention away from material disparities toward remediating supposed cultural and linguistic deficiencies of Latinx students. In this chapter, I examine the ways that this reconfigured racial logic informed professional debates surrounding bilingual education within the context of the Civil Rights movement.

Producing Deficiency

As mentioned in previous chapters, the mainstream social science approach to explaining racial inequalities in the 1960s was the culture of poverty theory, which suggested that multiple generations of poverty had created unique cultural deficiencies within racialized communities that prevented their social mobility. Language quickly rose to the top of these supposed cultural deficiencies, with "disadvantaged children" described as coming from homes that supposedly lacked rich linguistic input, leading these children to arrive to school already in need of intensive linguistic remediation.[4] It is here where discourses related to bilingual education emerged as a possibility for Spanish-speaking communities through a series of professional conferences focused primarily on the needs of Mexican Americans.[5] Produced within the discourse of the psychologically damaged racialized subject introduced previously, at the core of much of the discourse circulating at these conferences was the idea that English-only education damaged the self-esteem of Mexican American students. This can be seen in the 1966 National Education Association (NEA) conference in Tucson that was the first major professional educational conference to propose bilingual education as a solution to the challenges confronting Mexican American children.[6] The report produced as a result of the conference argued:

> The harm done the Mexican-American child linguistically is paralleled—perhaps even exceeded—by the harm done to him as a person. In telling him that he must not speak his native language, we are saying to him by implication that Spanish and the culture which it represents are of no worth. Therefore (it follows) the people who speak Spanish are of no worth. Therefore (it follows again) this particular child is of no worth. It should come as no surprise to us, then, that he develops a negative self-concept—an inferiority complex.[7]

A similar discourse was produced in the proceedings of the Texas Conference for the Mexican American held in San Antonio in 1967, which argued that:

> Conflict of cultures is one of the problems of the Spanish-speaking child—that we have failed to teach him about his culture, about the history of Mexico and Latin America, and about some of their important contributions to the world. . . . It is easy to conceive a six-year-old in trying to adjust to the new school environment who is told to forget the language he has learned at home and which he continues to use when he returns after school; naturally he senses something is wrong. . . . Not every six-year-old can cope with this kind of conflict. It is a conflict that easily develops into problems, educational and psychological, that too often leads to dropping out of school.[8]

In short, the major discourse circulating at these conferences acknowledged the legacy of racism that impacted the lives of Mexican American students, but suggested that the damage done to these children was at the level of their psyche as opposed to their material conditions.

This same discursive formation was also used to support bilingual education at a 1968 conference focused on the "special educational needs of urban Puerto Rican youth." Here, Bernard Friedman, an assistant superintendent in New York City schools, justified his support for bilingual education as helping to address "the identity problems of the young Puerto Rican and the social acceptability of his native tongue."[9] In a similar vein, Teodorina Bello, a representative of the New York State Education Department, described observing Puerto Rican children as experiencing shyness that could be overcome by "talking to them by using first the Spanish word."[10] These ideas were further emphasized by Antonia Pantoja, founder of Aspira, a Puerto Rican advocacy organization, in her remarks following the plenary where she insisted, "if you try to break the kid off from the roots he grew from, he will be damaged forever," insisting that the school system has made a concerted effort "to root out the sources of strength and pride that Puerto Rican children bring with them to school," with bilingual education being a viable strategy for challenging this dynamic.[11]

A major argument that emerged in these debates was that this psychological damage led Mexican American and Puerto Rican students to fail to become fully proficient in either Spanish or English. In the 1966 NEA survey of programs serving Mexican American students undertaken as part of their

Tucson conference, Mexican American children were described as "only nominally bilingual—not truly so" and were characterized as "speaking a language which is neither Spanish nor English but a mixture of the two—a kind of linguistic hybrid."[12] The report then went on to describe a range of bilingual education programs that the NEA considered to be "encouraging and exciting programs" to address these issues.[13] In this way, bilingual education was framed as compensatory education that would support Mexican American children in developing full proficiency in Spanish, which they purportedly lacked, that would then allow them to eventually increase their academic performance in English.

A prominent strand of this discursive formation focused on early childhood education, with the general concern being that unless remediation began early there would be permanent linguistic damage. This discourse can be found at a conference on early childhood bilingual education in 1967 where Vera John, the conference organizer, described "non-English speaking children who have been thrown into the ordinary school situation" as "premature bilingualists, meaning that their communicative competence in neither language has achieved a certain level of usefulness to them as speakers as well as thinkers." She went on to make the case for bilingual education by arguing that "when children have been forced to be concerned with the production of language in a language other than that in which they have been raised, at a time when they have not sufficiently developed language for the purpose of problem-solving and thought, then . . . their speaking competence in the secondary language becomes a secondary issue to the more fundamental one: how do you develop the full utilization of language in non-English-speaking children in America?"[14] This discourse can also be seen in the conference proceedings of the 1967 Texas Conference for the Mexican-American, where one of the papers argued that "the sober fact is that every disadvantaged year retards by so much the development of native capacities," insisting that "the native ability of a child cannot develop normally without adequate opportunity, and the severely disadvantaged home cannot offer that opportunity," and concluding that the only hope is to supplement the opportunities of the home as early in the child's life as outside help can be effective."[15] The author concluded that "extending education to the five-year-old is not enough for the children who have the double handicap of extremely limited developmental opportunities in the home and the necessity of learning a second language outside of the home.

For these children we must reach down to the four-year-old and perhaps even the three-year-old."[16]

One such preschool program that received a great deal of attention at these conferences was Good Samaritan, a bilingual preschool program for Spanish-speaking children developed in partnership with Kenneth Kramer, a psychology professor at Trinity College. This program began from the perspective that "as compared to middle-class children, [Spanish dominant] children are more restricted in language skills and lack the capacity for abstract language" and that "the child's language deprivation is his central educational handicap from which his other handicaps derive." With this in mind, the primary objective of Good Samaritan was to "remedy these language deficiencies by developing a preschool curriculum that focuses on increasing the language and communication skills of the Spanish-speaking child."[17] Suggesting that part of their linguistic deprivations comes from "limited adult-child interaction" and "restricted verbal experience—largely limited to informal and social interactions," the program also included parent meetings that had the goal of improving "child-rearing practices by providing parents with the opportunity to observe teacher-pupil interactions and then, through group discussions, to examine the role of the child and adult."[18] Good Samaritan was one of a range of bilingual education programs that emerged in the 1960s that would inform emerging debates about the BEA, examined in the next section.

Erasing Colonialism

In addition to harnessing momentum for his proposed legislation from the many professional conferences convened on the topic, Senator Yarborough held congressional hearings to gain more support for its passage. Two days of hearings were held in Washington, DC, with hearings subsequently held in Corpus Christ, Edinburg, Los Angeles, and New York City. All the speakers invited to testify were supportive of bilingual education, with many also involved in the professional educational organizations convening conferences on the topic. The only major points of disagreement that emerged were whether bilingual education could be sufficiently supported through existing funding sources and whether any newly proposed legislation should focus solely on Spanish speakers or be expanded to include all communities that spoke languages other than English. The House Committee on Education and Labor convened parallel hearings that had a similar pattern of overwhelming support for bilingual education, with the same disagreements.[19]

Senator Yarborough's original vision for what would become the BEA was for it to fund programs solely for Spanish speakers, with his primary focus being on advocating for funds for the American Southwest. He had two primary rationales for this. One rationale was that Spanish speakers were by far the largest bilingual group in the country. The other was the unique colonial history of the American Southwest. As he argued at the first congressional hearing on the BEA:

> If you take the Italians, Polish, French, Germans, Norwegians, or other non-English speaking groups, they made a definite decision to leave their old life and culture and come here to a new country and set up a way of life here in accordance with ours, and we assumed that they were consenting at that time to give up their language, too. That decision to come here carried with it a willingness to give up their language, everything. That wasn't true in the Southwest. We went in and took the people over, took over the land and culture. They had our culture superimposed on them. They did not consent to abandon their homeland and to come here and learn anew. They are not only the far more numerous group, but we recognize the fact that they are entitled to special consideration.[20]

In short, Senator Yarborough recognized the unique colonial history of the American Southwest and suggested that this relationship warranted specific interventions that differed from European immigrants. He maintained this stance throughout most of the congressional hearings, with his argument being that people were attempting to dilute the legislation by expanding it to include all non-English speakers.[21]

While Senator Yarborough's stance focused on the unique colonial history of the American Southwest, his proposed solutions were not focused on challenging the material consequences of this colonial relationship. Instead, his focus was on addressing the supposed psychological damage of this colonial relationship on the psyche of Spanish speakers living in the region. This can be seen in the ways that Senator Yarborough introduced the proposed legislation that I included as the introduction to this chapter. It was further emphasized in whom Senator Yarbrough invited to testify in the congressional hearings; he summarized their testimony in anticipation of the hearings as follows:

> Expert witnesses who will appear later before the subcommittee will comment on the psychological damage which such practices render unto millions of children. Even to a layman the injustice and harm of such practices are obvious. Unfortunately, this practice has all too often been the rule rather than the exception in the education of children from Spanish-speaking backgrounds.[22]

In short, while on one level Senator Yarborough appeared to adopt a materialist stance in acknowledging key differences between the colonial context that shaped the Mexican Americans in the American Southwest and the immigrant experiences of European immigrants, the core of his argument was that this colonial relationship had produced unique psychological damage for Mexican Americans that warranted special programs.

There was wide agreement with Yarborough's framing of the psychological damage of English-only schooling and the potential for bilingual education in fixing this damage. Yet, his insistence on focusing solely on Spanish speakers met strong opposition, further obscuring the materialist basis of racial inequities. One example of such resistance can be found in the congressional testimony of prominent bilingual education scholar Joshua Fishman. As he stated in his testimony in support of the BEA:

> I have no objection at all, quite the contrary, only the greatest admiration for your specification of Spanish in the bill. I only hope that there will be no approach which gets so frozen in this connection that the whole continent of submerged languages to which Spanish is related fails to be recognized. There are millions and millions of others that must feel that their recognition will come too, because they are wonderful Americans trying to contribute to America, and I am sure as the recognition to our Spanish-American citizens is long overdue, that it must come, so will the recognition for all the other creative language groups in the country.[23]

A similar sentiment was expressed by West Virginia Senator Jennings Randolph who, while being a sponsor of the BEA, still advocated that it be expanded beyond Spanish speakers, arguing that "I can see the need for moving beyond the Spanish-speaking problem to the problems of those with other basic languages. And I am not sure that in this legislation that broadening should not take place."[24] This point was reiterated by witness Alfred Gaarder, the chair of the foreign language section of the US Office of Education, in response to Senator Randolph's query into his stance on whether the legislation should include languages others than Spanish. In his reply he asserted that:

> The total problem is broader than that of the Spanish-speaking child alone, both the problem and the potential. At the very best, children who have a mother tongue other than English (such as the Polish children in my neighborhood) they have no problems with English, but they are being needlessly deprived of their Polish. At the worst, as in the case of many Spanish speakers and some others, not only are they being deprived of their Spanish but their lives are being damaged by our school policies regarding both languages. So I say it ought to be extended to make some larger coverage.[25]

In short, these comments conflate the experiences of Mexican Americans and other Spanish speakers with a general immigration experience in ways that erase the unique racialized experience of many of these communities in the United States. Their focus on supporting all bilingual communities left unaddressed the colonial relationship that Mexican Americans and other Spanish speakers such as Puerto Ricans had with the United States.

Also notable were the few discussions of Native American languages in the debate related to the BEA that focused primarily on Spanish speakers. Senator Yarborough acknowledged the "unique cultural problems" of Native Americans but suggested that their specific relationship to the United States required separate legislation than one focused on Mexican Americans and other Spanish speakers.[26] These sentiments were shared by Arizona Senator Paul Fannin, who sought to bring attention to the unique challenges confronting Native Americans, an interest he had because, as he noted, "we have more Indians in my State of Arizona than any other State in the United States." Yet, as with Yarborough's comments, he did not address the structural barriers confronting these communities as a legacy of white settler colonialism, but rather their unique "educational problems." He noted that, in contrast to Spanish speakers, indigenous people "do not have a general language," noting that "we have 15 tribes in our State and even in one tribe they may speak more than one language and it is a very limited language, as you know." Based on the supposed limited nature of these languages, he concluded that "we should do everything within our power to have special programs to take care of these needs, or a specific program assigned to this need."[27]

Beyond this explicit mention of the unique needs of Native Americans, in the few other moments where they were mentioned as part of the debate, they were included as part of a long list of bilingual communities. This can be seen in the testimony of US Education Commissioner Harold Howe II as he makes the case for why any proposed legislation should extend beyond Spanish-speakers:

> The primary beneficiaries of any nationwide bilingual education program would undoubtedly be Spanish-speaking children. But there are also other groups of children needing special programs whose home language is not Spanish. There are French-speaking children in Louisiana and near the Canadian border, children or oriental ancestry, and American Indians in significant numbers in various areas. We can expect that the number of children from other linguistic groups will increase in the next few years as a result of last year's liberalization of the Immigration Act. It is expected that larger numbers of children will be arriving from southern Europe that special programs will be necessary to meet their needs.[28]

He concluded that "I would prefer a broad approach to bilingual problems unless it becomes clear on the evidence of experts, people more expert than I, that the bilingual problems confronted by a particular group such as the Indians needs such special treatment that it should have special legislation."[29] This conflation of speakers of European languages with Native American languages obscured the specificities of the white settler colonialism suffered by Native American populations.

In this way, the discourses surrounding the BEA obscured the material consequences of colonialism in two ways. One way was through the conflation of Mexican and Puerto Rican communities with European immigrants in ways that obscured the colonial relationship between the United States and these communities forcefully incorporated into its territory. Another way was through the conflation of Native American communities with speakers of European languages (that would include many Mexican and Puerto Rican communities) in ways that obscured the fact that the United States was a white settler colonial society. The broader implication of this erasure of the materialist basis of colonialism was that the primary challenge confronting Spanish-speaking communities was framed as the same as the primary challenging confronting European immigrants and the same as the primary challenge confronting Native American communities—that they spoke a language other than English at home.

I would be remiss not to acknowledge the almost complete erasure of Asian Americans from these initial debates related to bilingual education, which is why they also do not appear in my analysis. They simply were not considered as relevant to the conversation. This is starkly illustrated by one of the few times that they are acknowledged in these debates, with William Carr, the executive secretary of the NEA, conflating them with European immigrants by insisting that "these immigrants have, on the whole, made a distinguished record. Nations overseas look at that record and they share in the glow of success which has been attained by their sons and daughters in North America." He contrasted this with "Latin American residents of the United States" and hoped that bilingual education could help them to "learn to read and write their own spoken language instead of suffering the functional illiteracy in both English and Spanish."[30] Here, we see the discursive emergence of what would eventually become the model minority stereotype that would position Asian Americans as culturally efficient, rather than culturally deficient, in ways that both erase the challenges confronted by this very diverse community and further blame African American and Latinx populations for their own continued marginalization.[31] While bilingual education programs serving the Asian American community would emerge using BEA funds and continue to thrive today,[32] these students continue to remain peripheral to debates surrounding bilingual education, often because of this model minority stereotype. The assumption was and continues to be that unlike Latinxs, Asian Americans do well academically and, therefore, don't need bilingual education or other remedial services to be successful.[33]

In short, at the core of debates surrounding the BEA was the simultaneous assertion that Spanish speakers should not receive special treatment in funds focused on promoting bilingual education, but did require special treatment in the types of bilingual education programs that should be offered to them. Specifically, the argument was that because of their unique colonial history in the United States, they had cultural and linguistic deficiencies that bilingual education was particularly well-positioned to remediate. This was connected to a more general discourse associated with the culture of poverty that, while first emerging in a study focused on Mexican society, had been taken up in the United States with a primary focus on the African American community. The psychologically damaged Black subject at the core of dominant discourse on the culture of poverty was then mobilized to frame Spanish speakers as similarly psychologically damaged. A key difference was that Spanish speakers were framed as having a native language that could be more fully developed to fix this psychological damage, with African Americans framed as having no legitimate native language that could be utilized in their remediation.[34] Yet, despite the shared sentiment that Spanish speakers had unique cultural and linguistic deficiencies, the bulk of the testimony in favor of the BEA favored a more general approach that would support all bilingual communities. This more general approach worked to obscure the unique colonial relationship of the American Southwest that Yarborough and others sought to bring attention to, while also obscuring the unique white settler colonial relations that have shaped the experiences of Native American communities. It is, therefore, not possible to understand the racialization of "Spanish speakers" within debates surrounding the BEA without understanding the anti-Black and white settler colonial logics that provide its foundation. It is also not possible to understand this outside of the emerging model minority stereotype that would be used to further perpetuate these deficit ideologies. Understanding these connections also helps us to better understand the ways that bilingual education activists who were in the process of being politically incorporated into the system were accepting a Faustian bargain that bestowed on them individual proximity to whiteness in exchange for accepting that Latinx and other racialized communities were fundamentally broken and needed to be fixed.

6
Accountable to Semilingualism

In 1976, El Centro de Estudios Puertorriqueños organized a panel on the Aspira Consent Decree, a binding agreement related to bilingual education that had recently been signed by the New York City Board of Education and Aspira of New York. Part of the discussion included an examination of the criteria that were being used to determine which students would be eligible for the new bilingual education programs that were being created in response to the Decree. Oscar García Rivera, the executive director of the Puerto Rican Legal Defense and Education Fund, described this procedure as based in

> [a]n interpretation that grew out of broader language that came out of the Consent Decree, which talked about children who because of their English language deficiencies could not learn effectively in English. . . . What the Court determined what that meant was that you first gave the children the test in English and if they fell below a certain level, which was determined by the Court to be the 20th percentile on the test then you could go on to the second part of the test in Spanish. If they did better, then they were considered to be qualified for the program.[1]

When the panel moderator Camille Garcia, coordinator of the National Puerto Rican Task Force on Educational Policy, asked about "the students who did not do well on the Spanish either," Mario Anglada, executive director of Aspira, provided the following answer:

> That was really one of our fears that children would not do well either in English or Spanish. . . . They have kind of a hybrid understanding of two languages none of them good enough to function in one of the languages. I think that brings a whole new issue about education and what can be done for those children.[2]

He estimated that between 10,000 and 12,000 of the students who were administered the two assessments fit into this category and concluded that

Becoming the System. Nelson Flores, Oxford University Press. © Oxford University Press 2024.
DOI: 10.1093/oso/9780197516812.003.0006

"we have to think about the issue of the children not being really able to function in any language in the complete sense" and suggested that this was an issue that required solutions that extended beyond the Consent Decree.[3]

Approximately thirty years later, I was a high school ESL teacher in the Bronx. Many of my students had been born in the United States and had been classified as English learners for their entire educational careers. They were referred to by the New York City Department of Education as "long-term English learners." I found myself using a similar discursive formation to explain why these students were still English learners after so many years—that they had failed to master academic language in either of their two languages and that these linguistic deficiencies lay at the root of their academic challenges. As I began my doctoral studies, I participated in a research project as both a teacher and a researcher that was designed to provide remediation to these students that would support the development of the purported academic language skills that they were lacking and that would improve their performance on standardized assessments.[4]

Both anecdotes point to the specter of semilingualism that I will examine in this chapter—that ghost of colonialism that suggests that racialized bilingual communities lack full proficiency in either of the two languages that they use daily. The first anecdote points to the role of the newly emerging accountability paradigm of the BEA and its associating assessment systems in institutionalizing the psychologically damaged racialized subject discussed in previous chapters as part of the reconfiguration from a biologized view of racial hierarchies to a cultural view of racial hierarchies. The second anecdote points to more contemporary raciolinguistic categories that have emerged as a result of this accountability paradigm and my own complicity as a Latino professional in reifying the racialization of my Latinx students in my teaching and research as part of my political incorporation into mainstream institutions.[5]

In this chapter, I examine the ways that the raciolinguistic ideologies made possible by the double erasure of colonialism, alongside the reification of anti-Blackness that undergirded the BEA, led to the development of a remedially oriented accountability system that relied on a dichotomous framing of students into those deemed eligible for bilingual education and those deemed ineligible for the program. I show how this remedial logic and dichotomous framing created an incentive for professional bilingual education advocates to define being "limited" enough to be eligible for the programs as broadly as possible to include the greatest number of students.

This led professional bilingual education advocates to double down on the raciolinguistic ideologies that lay at the core of the BEA, arguing that cultural and linguistic deficits of Latinxs and other racialized bilingual students—even those who were able to communicate in English—could be remedied through bilingual education.

The Dichotomous Framing of BEA Accountability

As examined in the previous chapter, debates surrounding the BEA suggested that the colonial relationship of the Mexican American and Puerto Rican communities to the United States had caused unique psychological damage to children within these communities, with bilingual education framed as one possible remedial program focused on fixing this damage. This remedial orientation provided the foundation for the accountability system that emerged in the 1970s to ensure that programs receiving BEA funds were meeting the policy's objectives. An accountability challenge that quickly arose was how to identify students who were deemed to have sufficient deficiencies to be eligible for the programs. The 1971 manual for BEA funding applicants noted, "in order to justify a bilingual education project, evidence must be presented that the other language is, in fact, the dominant language of the children to be served."[6] This determination had to include "the results of language tests in both English and the other language" that included "the identification of English language deficiencies" in order to "support the assumption that the proposed student participants have learning difficulties related to their language background which are not overcome by present programs."[7] The basic assumption ungirding the manual was that only certain students with sufficiently limited English proficiency were entitled to bilingual education programs and that schools and districts receiving BEA funds must have assessment data demonstrating that the students being served by the funded programs were students for whom such a program was justified. It was here where the dichotomous framing of students into bilingual students deemed eligible for bilingual education due to limited English proficiency and bilingual students deemed sufficiently proficient in English to not be eligible for the program emerged.

A related accountability challenge that quickly emerged was how to demonstrate that students deemed eligible for bilingual education programs were, in fact, making progress in these programs. According to the 1971 manual, "every local educational agency accepting a grant under Title VII will be held responsible for the achievement of specific objectives using certain procedures during a specified period of time," with these objectives "stated in terms of desired student performance."[8] According to the manual, this aspect of accountability "is largely dependent upon reliable and valid measurements of the project's accomplishments"[9] and must include "an assessment of progress in all project components—instruction, staff development, materials acquisition and development and community involvement—which interact in the effort to improve student performance"[10] through reliance on "a variety of instruments, both formal and informal, teacher-constructed and standardized, to measure the progress of the project toward the stated objectives."[11] In this way, BEA accountability not only entailed demonstrating that students participating in bilingual education programs were sufficiently limited in their English, but also entailed demonstrating that students who were deemed eligible for bilingual education were making sufficient academic progress and sufficient progress toward the English-language proficiency determined to be high enough for them to be able to enter mainstream classrooms.

The need to identify students deemed to have sufficiently limited English proficiency to justify being in bilingual education, coupled with the need to monitor their growth in English-language proficiency, was complemented by a focus on the home-language proficiency of the students. The question of whether Latinx students deemed as limited English proficient had sufficient proficiency in their home language to be able to thrive in bilingual education programs was treated as an empirical question. Building on verbal deprivation theory, the assumption was that because of the psychological damage of racism, it was possible for Latinx students to be limited not only in their English-language proficiency in ways that warranted special language programs, but also in their Spanish-language proficiency in ways that suggested that these students should not be receiving bilingual education. The 1971 BEA manual offered the first glimpse into the emergence of this raciolinguistic category that would subsequently be taken up in the Aspira Consent Decree panel described above. In particular, the manual cautioned districts and schools to be aware of "instances in which children speak English imperfectly because of a foreign language background but do not speak the foreign language themselves at home," noting that this "would justify a program in English as a second language, but not a bilingual program." That is, the manual supposed that there might be students who were limited

English proficient who did not even speak a language other than English who would be entitled to ESL services, but not to bilingual education.

The logic that undergirded this BEA accountability was further strengthened through the courts. More pressure to develop mechanisms to identify students eligible for bilingual education and/or other special language programs emerged in response to the 1974 *Lau v. Nichols* Supreme Court decision that ruled that simply providing the same facilities, textbooks, teachers, and curriculum for students who do not understand English violated Title VI of the Civil Rights Act of 1964 that prohibited discrimination based on race, color, or national origin.[12] The *Lau* Remedies that were released by the Office for Civil Rights in response to the court decision mandated that schools administer a home-language survey to identify students whose primary or home language was a language other than English and if so to determine whether they were eligible for bilingual education and/or other special language programs. For the purposes of identifying students for further evaluating, the Lau remedies defined the primary or home language as other than English if one of the three criteria were met: (a) the student's first acquired language is other than English; (b) the language most often spoken by the student is other than English; or (c) the language most often spoken in the student's home is other than English, regardless of the language spoken by the student.[13] If the answer to any of these criteria was yes, students needed to be further evaluated to determine whether they were eligible for bilingual education and/or other special language programs, with a key dimension especially relevant for bilingual education programs being home-language assessments "to determine whether the student speaks it fluently."[14]

While the *Lau* Remedies themselves only identified "a test of language dominance as a third criterion" that could be used in cases of conflicting information between what is documented in the home and the school, such as a "student [who] speaks Spanish at home, but English with classmates at lunch,"[15] school districts became increasingly reliant on the use of standardized language-proficiency assessments to dichotomize students as eligible or ineligible for special language programs, with most districts receiving BEA funds relying on them for determinations of eligibility for bilingual education programs by the end of the 1970s.[16] By 1980, language assessments were being described as "the first step in providing appropriate instruction to language minority students. It determines which students would be at a disadvantage in English-medium classrooms and how proficient they are in their native languages. It thus determines their eligibility for publicly funded bilingual education and special English programs."[17] Advocates for bilingual education who were interested in ensuring that the greatest number of students possible were eligible for these programs and were permitted to remain in these programs for as long as possible sought to make the cutoff scores for these assessments as high as possible. As I will examine below, these efforts worked to reinforce the broader discursive move from biological to cultural explanations for racial hierarchies into bilingual education policy and practice in ways that continue to frame these programs in the contemporary context.

The Emergence of Semilingualism in Bilingual Education Policy

As described above, the need to identify students deemed eligible for bilingual education emerged as a major debate after the passage of the BEA. Heidi Dulay and Marina Burt, two researchers working with districts in California, posited three distinct subgroups of limited-English-proficient (LEP) students: (1) non-English-superior students who were more proficient in their home language; (2) English-superior students who, though limited in English, were more proficient in English than in their home language; and (3) equally limited students whose proficiency in their home language and in English were limited to an equal extent. These designations were determined based on language-proficiency assessments, with students "considered superior in one of the languages tested if he or she scored one full level higher in one language than the other" and "students who scored in the same level in both languages and are within the range of limited proficiency are equally limited."[18] For Dulay and Burt, non-English-superior LEP students should receive bilingual education that included "basic academic instruction through the home language . . . and a transition period before the student transfers out of home-language-medium classes to the regular school curriculum," while English-superior students should have English "used as the medium of academic instruction and . . . receive special English instruction."[19] They argued that "equally limited bilinguals who speak *English* at home would best be instructed in *English*, while those who speak another language at home might benefit more from instruction through their language."[20]

These recommendations conflicted with the desires of proponents of bilingual education to ensure that the maximum number of students possible be deemed eligible for these programs. They sought an alternative explanation that could be used to justify making these programs available to students from the other two subgroups as well. One prominent alternative position was developed by bilingual education scholar Jim Cummins. He argued that "because parents are ashamed of their cultural background or feel they speak an inferior dialect of L1, they may not strongly encourage children to develop L1 skills in the home." He added that this resulted in a household dynamics where "they may communicate with the child only when necessary or use a mixture of L1 and L2 in the home," leaving the child "without a conceptual basis for learning L1 in an L2-only school situation," leading to "low levels of proficiency (e.g. reading skills) in both languages."[21] In short, the argument was that the legacy of racism had produced linguistic deprivation in Latinx households, leading children to not full attain proficiency in either Spanish or English.

Cummins originally described this phenomenon as *semilingualism*, which he defined as "the linguistic competence, or lack of it, of individuals who have had contact with two languages since childhood without adequate training or stimulation in either. As a consequence, these individuals know two languages poorly and do not attain the same levels as native speakers in either language."[22] He would further refine his framework in the 1980s through the introduction of *Basic Interpersonal Communication Skills* (BICS), which he defined as "the 'visible' language proficiencies of pronunciation, vocabulary, grammar, which are manifested in everyday interpersonal communicative situations" and *Cognitive Academic Language Proficiency* (CALP), which he defined as "language proficiency required to manipulate or reflect upon these surface features outside of immediate interpersonal contexts."[23] He used this framing as a starting point for justifying bilingual education programs based on the assumption that

> [t]he relatively greater success of vernacular education in minority language situations is due, partly at least, to the fact that certain aspects of the minority child's linguistic knowledge may not be fully developed on entry to school. Thus, some children may have only limited access to the cognitive-linguistic operations necessary to assimilate L2 and develop literacy skills in that language.[24]

Framing it within the BICS and CALP dichotomy, he argued that "to the extent that instruction in Lx is effective in promoting cognitive/academic proficiency in Lx, transfer of this proficiency to Ly will occur provided there is adequate exposure to Ly (either in school or environment) and adequate motivation to learn Ly."[25]

Putting this all together, Cummins argued that "the success of bilingual programs derives from the fact that children and parents are encouraged to take pride in their own language and culture as well as from the fact that schools try to build on the cognitive and linguistic abilities which children bring to school," adding that "minority language groups that tend to perform poorly under conditions of home-school language switch appear to be characterized by ambivalence towards both their own culture and the majority culture."[26] Based on this framing, Cummins argued that the assertion that "English-superior" LEP students should not be eligible for bilingual education focuses "only on surface manifestations of language" and "ignores the sociocultural determinants of minority children's school failure."[27] Instead, Cummins advocated that any assessment used to determine who was eligible for bilingual education programs should assess English CALP skills, as this might be a good indicator of some of the sociocultural determinants at play in determining who would benefit from bilingual education.

By 1980, frameworks for developing these standardized language-proficiency assessments were beginning to be developed. Importantly, these frameworks had been created within the existing transitional logic of needing to identify students eligible for bilingual education programs and eligible for reclassification out of bilingual education. The question that dominated discussions was how standardized language proficiency assessments could help determine "*who* should enter bilingual education programs, *why* they should be there, and *how* to identify them," coupled with questions related to "*who* should exit from bilingual programs, *why* they should exit, and *how* to identify students who should exit."[28] This led to a redefinition of language proficiency for bilingual Latinxs and other bilinguals to one that encompassed all of the necessary linguistic competencies needed to engage in grade-level content in English.

An example of one project that sought to refine this new conceptualization of language proficiency was the Resources for Developing a Student Placement System for Bilingual Program funded by the US Office of Education. A major component of this project was the development of the

Language Skills Framework (LSF) that identified 285 different language skills "to assist Title VII projects in developing and implementing their own system(s) for selecting students for Title VII program participation, periodically reviewing students, determining when it is appropriate to transfer students to other instructional programs, and providing the necessary follow-up assistance to transferred students."[29] The framework emphasized the importance of determining "if a student has sufficient receptive and productive command over spoken English and its use to be able to function in an all-English-medium classroom at his appropriate grade level." This included classroom interaction skills "that enable the student to interact appropriately with the teacher during classroom instruction," with proficiency in these activities representing "an important segment of information for making entry and reclassification decisions."[30] The framework also emphasized the importance of assessing reading proficiency "based on the content and skills in the major reading programs that are used in schools throughout the country"[31] and assessing writing proficiency based on an "analysis and specification of the actual writing skills taught by the writing programs that are used in classrooms."[32]

In this way, the remedial orientation of the BEA, coupled with the linguistic demands of mainstream classrooms, led Latinxs and other bilingual students to be framed as "limited" in their English proficiency and perhaps also in their home language if they could not demonstrate the ability to effectively engage in grade-level classroom interactions, reading and writing in English or their home language. It was this inability to demonstrate proficiency in grade-level content in either English or Spanish that was first referred to as semilingualism and then as BICS and CALP. While the terminology over the past several decades has shifted, as I will examine in the next section, the specter of semilingualism remains prominent in contemporary discussions of bilingual education policy in ways that continue to propose linguistic solutions to complex social problems.

Tracing the Specter of Semilingualism in Contemporary Bilingual Education Policy

From 1980 until the present, the gradual movement has been to broaden the definition of what counts as "limited" English proficiency in ways that have expanded the number of children classified as eligible for bilingual education and/or other special language programs. This expanding definition of who counted as "limited" enough to be eligible for these programs occurred alongside a broader national conversation that began to focus on raising standards for all students with the publication of *A Nation at Risk*. In both cases, standardized assessments became an integral tool for ensuring that students were introduced to higher expectations. While the general conversation focused on developing challenging assessments that would ensure all students mastered knowledge identified by policymakers as necessary for their future success,[33] the language-specific conversation focused on developing more challenging English-language proficiency assessments that would ensure that students were appropriately identified as in need of bilingual education and/or other special language programs and that would ensure that they remained in these programs until they would be able to successfully engage in grade-level content in English.[34] Both conversations located the root of racial inequalities in low standards and framed the solution as increasing standards in order to narrow the achievement gap.

The passage of *No Child Left Behind* (NCLB) marked the official end of the BEA. Indeed, it also marked the complete erasure of the term "bilingual" from federal policy.[35] Yet, the remedial orientation that undergirded the BEA, coupled with the general standards-based reform movement, continued to lead to the broadening of the category of students deemed sufficiently limited in English to justify special language programs. Continuing the trend of raising standards for all students, NCLB stated that students officially classified as English learners should be held to the same academic standards as the rest of the student population.[36] The primary way that NCLB sought to ensure this outcome was through the disaggregation of achievement data on state general-content assessments in determining whether states, districts, and schools made adequate yearly progress toward the ambitious goal of having all students, including those officially classified as English learners, scoring as proficient by 2014.[37] Alongside disaggregating academic performance as part of the general accountability system, NCLB also required states, districts, and schools to develop annual measurable achievement outcomes focused specifically on the English-language development of students classified as English learners across the four domains of listening, speaking, reading, and writing.[38] In addition, NCLB mandated that states develop English-language proficiency standards that were aligned with state content standards, leading to the development of more challenging English-language proficiency standards and assessments.[39] As a result, more potential "limited" English-proficient students were classified as actually "limited" and once classified had to meet increasingly higher standards to be reclassified as fully English proficient. In the context of bilingual education, more of these students were also classified as not being fully proficient in either English or their home language, with some districts referring to these students as "non-nons."[40]

It is within this context that the raciolinguistic category of "long-term English learner" (LTEL) had risen to discursive prominence by the time I entered the classroom. Since I have left the classroom, this raciolinguistic category has become even further institutionalized, with California officially incorporating the category into state law in 2012 and the federal government in the *Every Student Succeeds Act* (ESSA) in 2015. An influential report written by Laurie Olsen, published by the advocacy organization Californians Today, played an instrumental role in getting the LTEL category institutionalized in California and bringing it into the broader national conversation. In this report, Olsen suggested that the primary reason for their academic challenges was "the impact of weak English language skills and not having received targeted language development" leading to "limited attainment of all subject matter."[41] Relying on the social versus academic language dichotomy that is often used interchangeably with the BICS/CALP dichotomy, she described the vocabulary that they used to be "an 'imprecise' social language" that exhibited "fossilized features of language based upon the home language system superimposed with English vocabulary." She noted that "while it is expressive and functional in many social situations, it is not a strong foundation for the language demands of academic work in Standard English."[42] She added that "in order to engage with the academic demands of secondary school curriculum, they must learn more complex syntax, richer oral language, and the specialized vocabulary needed to understand academic text and participate in classroom discussions."[43] Based on this description, Olsen called for a focus on academic language development (ALD) that "focuses on powerful oral language development, explicit literacy development, instruction in the academic uses of English, high quality writing, extensive reading of relevant texts, and an emphasis on academic language and complex vocabulary,"[44] alongside home-language instruction that includes "explicit literacy instruction aligned to the literacy standards in English and designed for skill transfer across languages."[45]

As can be seen, the discursive construction of the LTEL category shares many of the underlying logics that produced the concept of semilingualism and is still produced within the dichotomous framing of language into BICS, or social language that these students are purported to have mastered, and CALP, or academic language that these students are purported to have not mastered. While there is a continued nod to sociocultural determinants, the primary focus of this broader analysis continues to be on the idea that students lack full mastery over the language skills deemed necessary for academic success. As a result, the solutions proposed are those focused on linguistic remediation. There is little discussion of the fact that many of these students go to poorly resourced schools and reside in segregated neighborhoods that have been produced by generations of racist public policy. There are few questions raised about the validity of standardized assessments that are far removed from the lived experience of these students in determining their language proficiency. There is no reflection on the ways that ideologies of languagelessness that call into question the language practices of racialized communities have a long history where they have been continuously used to dehumanize these communities as part of the justification for their continued exploitation.[46]

The legacy of this long colonial history can be seen in comparisons that Olsen makes to other racialized students who are also struggling academically. Specifically, she notes that the test scores of LTELs "might look similar to struggling adolescent native speakers and they also struggle with academic language and comprehending academic texts," also noting that they "share much in common with other Standard English learners—the mix of English vocabulary superimposed on the structure of the heritage language and the use of a dialect of English that differs from academic English."[47] Here we can see the underlying raciolinguistic ideology that produces the LTEL as having roots in the anti-Blackness and white settler colonial logics that undergird the Standard English Learner category. This underlying logic can been seen in a Standard English Learner linguistic screener used in Los Angeles that seeks to identify students who "would particularly benefit from mainstream English language development."[48] The screener provides separate lists of "African American linguistic features," "Hawaiian American linguistic features," and "Mexican American linguistic features." Each list includes approximately twenty sentences that are represented in Standard English and the respective nonstandard racialized variety, highlighting the particular linguistic features that distinguish between the two varieties. The emphasis of the screener is to identify students deemed to be deficient enough in their Standard English abilities to warrant remediation that would focus on correcting their linguistic deficiencies. Suggesting that the primary challenge of African American and Native Hawaiian students is dialectal variation continues the erasure of the anti-Blackness and white settler colonialism that undergirded the BEA and subsequent language education policies. The inclusion of Mexican American students on this list shows the ways that the racialization of Latinxs is produced within the broader foundational anti-Blackness and white settler colonialism of US society. It is also noteworthy that there are no screeners that could be used for white students. The assumption seems to be that they would never need such linguistic remediation.

Testing Accountability

Within the context of community control in the 1960s, a major rallying cry was for schools to be held accountable to the communities that they serve. While initially this accountability was conceptualized within calls for community-based governance and democratic participation, the term "accountability" has increasingly become associated with student performance on standardized assessments. While this shift has typically been associated with the publication of *A Nation at Risk* in 1983 and the path that this laid for the passage of NCLB in 2001, BEA accountability marked earlier federal involvement in shaping educational accountability and offered a prelude of what was to come. Specifically, the raciolinguistic ideologies that undergirded the deficit frameworks that were used to make sense of Latinx student performance on standardized language-proficiency assessments paralleled the raciolinguistic ideologies that would be taken up to explain the performance of all racialized students on general content assessments. The idea was that these students performed poorly on these assessments because of cultural and linguistic deficiencies, and the way to remediate these deficiencies was to raise expectations by increasing standards. These discourses worked to obscure the material basis of racism and instead refocus attention to fixing racialized students and their communities.

To be clear, the point of examining the historical development of accountability is not to blame professional bilingual education advocates who may have felt forced to accept the terms of the debate in order to ensure that bilingual education was made available to as many students as possible. Nor is it intended to blame contemporary advocates who continue to rely on this framing, especially since I myself relied on them as a teacher and am no doubt complicit in continuing to reproduce them as a Latino professional who is often pressured to accept deficit frameworks of Latinx and other racialized communities as part of gaining proximity to whiteness and the individual benefits that it might bestow on me. Instead, it is intended to denaturalize this framing by pointing to the sociohistorical context of its emergence as a way of calling into question the foundational assumptions of raciolinguistic categories such as LTEL.[49] It is intended to bring renewed attention to the material basis of white supremacy and the importance of working to account for this material basis in how we discuss issues of bilingual education.[50] Even more importantly, it is intended to bring attention to the complicity of these raciolinguistic categories in not only reifying the racialization of Latinxs, but also further entrenching anti-Blackness and white settler colonialism into educational debates. An accountability system premised on the supposed cultural and linguistic deficits of racialized communities will never address the root causes of racial inequities and will always serve to further maintain them.

7
Becoming an Entrenched Bureaucracy

In 1971, Rhody McCoy, the former unit administrator of the Ocean Hill–Brownsville community-control demonstration district, reflected on the many factors that led to its demise. A major culprit that he identified was the educational bureaucracy that structured the experiment in a way that ensured its failure. As he argued, "the giant bureaucracy . . . comprised the heart of this strategy of oppression . . . by perpetuating the rationale which supported the old system,"[1] describing these bureaucracies as having "been perverted from institutions which serve the people into bastardized servants of the power elite"[2] and thereby enforcing a "policy of educational genocide"[3] designed to keep "the blacks docile in concentration camps."[4] Based on this critical analysis of the educational bureaucracy, he insisted that "the mere introduction of black faces into the various levels of the educational bureaucracy, even at the top of the bureaucracy, does not affect the quality of education offered to black children."[5] This perspective was shared by Luis Fuentes, the first Puerto Rican principal in New York City who was hired by McCoy to work in Ocean Hill–Brownsville, and who created a bilingual program to serve its sizable Puerto Rican population. In his reflections on the demise of the experiment, he described the educational bureaucracy as "neocolonial"[6] and as a "jello monster" because of the way "we all seem to disappear inside it."[7] For these advocates for community control, the educational bureaucracy was dangerous and had the potential to co-opt racialized community struggles in ways that maintained the white supremacist status quo.

In contrast to this perspective, Albert Shanker, the president of the United Federation of Teachers, painted supporters of the Ocean Hill–Brownsville experiment as extremists who "desired a confrontation,"[8] which he contrasted with "the real community in Ocean Hill [who] never turned up at any of the rallies called by these militants."[9] He blamed this extremism on "the attempt on the part of civil officials and foundation executives to accommodate to the most militant and separatist elements in the black community in order to de-fuse what they consider to be an explosive situation."[10] Painting these extremists as "a sort of hoodlum element,"[11] he warned people that the

Becoming the System. Nelson Flores, Oxford University Press. © Oxford University Press 2024.
DOI: 10.1093/oso/9780197516812.003.0007

consequences of allowing them to prevail in Ocean Hill–Brownsville would mean "that there will be people in their own communities who will see this as a model of success and move in and take over these institutions."[12] For Shanker, community control represented an existential threat to the fabric of US society, with the role of the educational bureaucracy being to minimize this threat, as opposed to supporting its continued growth.

In 1995, echoing earlier discourses utilized by community-control advocates, Sally Peterson, an educator participating in an anti-bilingual education conference organized by the Center for Educational Opportunity, painted bilingual education as an entrenched bureaucracy. She argued that

> advocates of bilingual education will tell you their main goal is to teach English to non-English-speaking children. But I tell you their primary purpose is to perpetuate a seriously flawed teaching method so that the bureaucracy that supports it can sustain itself. Their livelihoods depend on promoting the myth that children taught in one language—80 percent of it Spanish—will learn English.[13]

For Peterson, the increasing bureaucratization of bilingual education had produced a professional class of Latinx bureaucrats who were not only out of touch with the communities they purported to represent, but also had a vested interest in keeping these communities "alienated from the rest of our society."[14] The year prior to the conference, in response to a Latinx parent protest against the state's mandated bilingual education policy, Joseph Ramos, the co-chair of the North Jersey Bilingual Council, was quoted as asking, "why would we require parents unfamiliar with our educational system to make such a monumental decision when we are trained to make those decisions."[15] For Ramos, in line with Shanker's earlier sentiment, the primary role of educational bureaucracy was to keep politics of out US schools by relying on dispassionate expertise, as opposed to the uninformed desires of communities.

As can be seen, the 1960s to the 1990s witnessed a political reconfiguration of the relationship between racialized communities and educational bureaucracies. In line with this general shift, by the end of the 1970s, bilingual education activists had been transformed from advocates for more community control and less powerful centralized educational bureaucracies to professionalized workers reliant on these very bureaucracies to protect bilingual education and often maintain their own salaries. What remained consistent was the racializing imagery that was used by bilingual education opponents that, in line with Albert Shanker's criticism of community-control advocates, framed its proponents as out-of-touch militants who were more interested in preserving their own power than in supporting the communities they purported to be representing.

This chapter traces the political mechanisms that led to the increased bureaucratization of bilingual education. Specifically, I examine how the neoliberal assault on bureaucracies can be understood as a reaction to the increasing racial diversity of federal, state, and local bureaucracies and the ways that critics of bilingual education were able to build on and extend the neoliberal critique of government bureaucracies through reliance on long-standing racializing discourses that framed bilingual education activists as dangerous militants working to undermine the unity of US society. I end by examining the ways that this rhetoric was deployed in a successful effort to ban bilingual education in California in 1998, with bilingual education activists characterized as the incompetent and out-of-touch educational bureaucrats that bilingual education activists of the previous generations had mobilized to resist in struggles for community control of schools.

The Bureaucratization of Bilingual Education

A seminal moment in the creation of the federal bilingual educational bureaucracy was a 1970 memorandum by the Department of Health, Education, and Welfare that mandated that school districts take affirmative steps to support students who were identified as limited-English-proficient.[16] This memorandum led the Department to request and be granted permission to support the *Lau v. Nichols* petitioners as *amicus curiae*, which offered the stamp of approval of the US Supreme Court to the stance articulated in the 1970 Memorandum.[17] In response to the *Lau* decision, Congress passed the Equal Educational Opportunities Act of 1974, which included a provision institutionalizing the 1970 Memorandum and the *Lau* decision into federal law by decreeing that all school districts must "take action to overcome language barriers that impede equal participation by its students in its instructional program."[18]

The federal bilingual education bureaucracy was further expanded through the 1975 *Lau* Remedies. While the *Lau* Remedies were created as guidelines rather than mandates, they essentially became de facto compliance standards that the Office for Civil Rights (OCR) used to determine whether school districts were respecting the civil rights of their students who were determined to have limited English proficiency. Their strong preference for bilingual education, especially at the elementary school level, significantly limited state and local discretion, with OCR having the authority to mandate the creation of compliance plans where states and school districts had to lay out the corrective action they would be taking to address any civil rights violations.[19] Between 1975 and 1980, OCR carried out nearly 600 national-origin compliance reviews, leading to the negotiation of 359 school-district *Lau* plans by July 1980.[20] OCR was supported by the Office of Education's Division of Equal Educational Opportunity that funded nine *Lau* Centers that were charged with helping school districts design language education programs that were in compliance with federal guidelines.[21]

The federal bilingual educational bureaucracy continued to expand through the 1974 reauthorization of the BEA that established the Office of Bilingual Education (OBE).[22] The OBE was primarily charged with capacity building which included "teacher training efforts, development and dissemination of materials, and the development of model programs which could be replicated or adopted in other school districts," with the goal of providing "local school districts with the human and material resources needed to operate bilingual programs."[23] While this capacity building was intended to support districts, it also further strengthened the BEA accountability system in ways that also constrained the decisions of districts receiving BEA funds concerning what they could do with those funds.[24] The 1974 BEA also created a National Advisory Council for Bilingual Education that consisted of experts in bilingual education who were charged with advising the OBE, along with the broader federal bilingual education bureaucracy, on matters related to bilingual education.[25] Together, the OBE and the National Advisory Council sought to further expand the federal bureaucracy supporting bilingual education.

These efforts to expand the federal bureaucracy supporting bilingual education can be found in the first report the National Advisory Council submitted to the OBE. A primary recommendation of this report was a call for more federal funding to assist states in developing bilingual education programs. They advocated a carrot-and-stick approach that would offer states working toward the development of bilingual education "greater Federal capacity-building and support funds under title VII," with states that have not moved in the direction of bilingual education not receiving federal funds "until they take positive steps toward servicing children of limited English-speaking ability in bilingual-multicultural programs."[26] They also recommended that "States presently requiring public and/or nonpublic school instruction be exclusively in English not be considered eligible for Title VII funds after fiscal 1981."[27] In line with this strong support of an active federal involvement in promoting bilingual education, the Council also called on the OBE to "assume the role of an active promoter of bilingual-multicultural education, presenting convincing informational material, especially to individuals and key influencers in States which have not accepted bilingual-multicultural education as a viable approach, and making technical assistance and training available to responsible official." The Council insisted that the OBE should be making the case for bilingual education "not only as the best educational approach for students of limited English-speaking ability, but as a viable approach for all students."[28] Many in the OBE were sympathetic to this position, with one senior program specialist calling for "a national plan which would provide a framework both for federal policies and activities at the state and local level . . . and make explicit the basis for policy directives."[29]

In line with this perspective, the 1970s saw a massive expansion of the federal bilingual education bureaucracy. Over the course of the decade, the budget for federal bilingual education programs went from $7.5 million to $160 million.[30] By 1976, the US Commissioner of Education reported "16 different sources of help for language minority students in the Office of Education [that] span the spectrum of elementary and secondary, postsecondary, occupational, adult, and vocational education, and education for the handicapped."[31] Similar expansion occurred in state- and local-level educational bureaucracies, with 30 states having enacted bilingual education legislation and 22 of these states providing their own funds to support the expansion of these programs, which by the 1980s covered twice as many students as federally funded programs did.[32]

This culminated in the newly formed Department of Education efforts to formalize the *Lau* Remedies into policies and procedures that all states and districts would be expected to adhere to in 1980. Department officials worked to balance the criticism on one side that the proposed requirements would be too prescriptive and costly and would work to undermine state and local discretion with criticism from the other side that too much flexibility might lead to civil rights violations in the name of local discretion.[33]

Coming just a few months before the presidential election, the proposed regulations became a campaign issue, with the Reagan campaign citing them as an example of federal overreach that he would eliminate, along with the new Department of Education, if elected.[34] While he never did eliminate the Department of Education, he did withdraw the proposed regulations and oversaw drastic cuts to federal funding for bilingual education, including the dismantling of civil rights monitoring of states and districts in relation to bilingual education.[35] This was part of the broader neoliberal turn that came alongside Reagan's rise to power, with race being a key mechanism in the shaping of this agenda.

The Neoliberal Assault on Bilingual Education

Foundational to Reagan's neoliberal agenda was the basic premise that the War on Poverty and the institutionalization of the demands of the Civil Rights movement had developed a self-interested federal bureaucracy that was more invested in its own preservation as an employer of people from racialized communities than in improving the lives of the communities they purported to represent. Appropriating earlier community-control critiques of government bureaucracies, the major argument made was that the federal bureaucracy had increased the dependency of racialized communities, contributing to their continued moral decline while also undermining local control.[36] In response to this narrative, racialized community activists found themselves defending the very bureaucratic structures that many of them had once critiqued within the context of community control.[37] What remained consistent were the ways that these racialized community activists were depicted by their opponents—as out-of-touch, dangerous militants bent on destroying the fabric of US society.

This dynamic can be seen in the debates related to the Reagan administration's assault on the federal bilingual education bureaucracy that began with the elimination of the *Lau* Remedies and was further strengthened by the 1984 announcement of Education Secretary William Bennett's Bilingual Education Initiative. Framed in terms of local control, this initiative sought to provide states and districts with more flexibility in terms of how they met the needs of students determined to be limited-English-proficient by further weakening OCR oversight and incorporating into the BEA funds for English-only alternatives to bilingual education.[38]

The National Council de la Raza (NCLR) condemned this move by the Reagan administration, arguing that

> an increased reliance on English-only programs by the federal government is a powerful message to state houses and local boards of education. It is likely that a move to abandon bilingual education at the federal level will make it more difficult for many states and local districts to operate bilingual program.[39]

Based on the hostility of Secretary Bennett to bilingual education, the NCLR also called for more congressional oversight over the Department of Education's administration of BEA funds and monitoring of civil rights policies as they related to students determined to have limited English proficiency.[40] In this way, the NCLR saw increasing bureaucratic oversight as the main mechanism for defending bilingual education.

A key mechanism that the Reagan administration used to counteract these efforts was to recycle the racialized imagery utilized by Albert Shanker and other predominantly white critics of community control that framed racialized community activists as dangerous militants seeking to exploit government resources to promote a separatist agenda. In terms of bilingual education, this can be seen in Secretary Bennett's nominees to the National Advisory Council on Bilingual Education, who not only opposed bilingual education but whose opposition to it relied on racializing imagery that included referring to bilingual education as the "new Latin hustle" and as a plot on the part of Latinx leaders to keep children in "linguistic bondage."[41] This depiction of bilingual education activists would come into increasingly prominence throughout the 1980s as part of the broader backlash against the institutionalized gains of the Civil Rights movement.[42] In the next section, I examine some of these critiques before examining the ways that they were successfully taken up as part of efforts to outlaw bilingual education in California in the late 1990s.

Paving the Way to Banning Bilingual Education

The Reagan administration's assault on the federal bilingual education bureaucracy connected to the emergence of a broader discursive formation that came to prominence in the late 1970s and 1980s, which painted

Latinx activists working to promote bilingual education as out-of-touch militant bureaucrats who had an active political interest in keeping Latinx communities from successfully assimilating into US society through "affirmative ethnicity."[43] While framed in terms of ethnicity, at the core of this discursive formation was the racialization of Latinidad that framed it as both inherently foreign and dangerous. One stark example of such a framing can be found in a widely circulated critique of bilingual education published in 1983 by a Los Angeles educator who contrasted "Americans" whom he described as "reluctant to criticize [bilingual education] for fear of displaying ignorance" with "the ethnic politician" for whom it is "politically advantageous . . . if immigrants continue to rely on their native language . . . since dependence on the home language tends to isolate the group and make it more manipulable."[44] For this person, "ethnic politicians" were not "American," and their increasing power in educational bureaucracies posed an existential threat to US society.

These critiques of bilingual education continued into the 1990s, with one prominent critique published by Peter Duignan who was a senior fellow at the Hoover Institute, a prominent conservative think tank. Duignan identified the emergence of the federal bilingual education bureaucracy with the development of the Inter-Agency Committee on Mexican American Affairs in 1967, along with the passage of the BEA in 1968, which he argued "Hispanic activists, especially militant Chicanos, have seized . . . to get Spanish-language instruction."[45] He also pointed to the ways that Latinx people with expertise in bilingual education were appointed to staff positions in a range of federal bureaucracies, including the Civil Rights Commission, the Equal Employment Opportunity Commission, and the Office of Education. He characterized these Latinx federal bureaucrats as "self-styled progressives [who] formed an informal but powerful lobby committed to institutional change."[46] He argued that these federal bureaucrats were able to successfully expand bilingual education "from a small program in 1968 to educate Mexican American children" with spending in the range of $7.5 million to "an $8 billion a year industry."[47] He argued that this increased funding "had created a new political lobby of bilingual supervisors, aides, counselors, instructors, publishers of textbooks, producers of films, tapes, and other aids, and professors in education providing courses in bilingual education."[48]

In line with the racialization of Latinidad that framed the category as perpetually foreign and dangerous, Duignan framed bilingual education activists as working to undermine the integrity of US society. In particular, he characterized professional bilingual education bureaucrats as "militant Hispanic separatists"[49] who aspire "to Hispanicize and to capture federal funds for schools"[50] to support "a program to Hispanicize, not Americanize, Spanish speakers."[51] He argued that these militants, "guided by the principle of 'cultural maintenance,' want Hispanic-surnamed children to continue to be taught Spanish language and culture and English only as a second language."[52] Focusing specifically on the American Southwest, he argued that "Mexican American activists reject assimilation, insist on bilingualism and multiculturalism, and lay claim to Southwest America as belonging to Mexico!" arguing that "their message is not pushing assimilation but rather the protection of Spanish language and culture and the theme that the Southwest United States belongs to the descendants of Mexicans who lost the war of 1848."[53] He argued that such a vision sought to create "linguistic enslaves" that "divide America"[54] through demands for "official recognition as groups and proportional representation," which he suggested were "requirements incompatible with the operation of a free market."[55] Illustrating the connection between the racialization of Latinidad and anti-Black logics, he attributed the rise of these efforts to undermine the free market to the fact that "Mexican and Asian activists have learned from the civil rights struggles conducted by black Americans and thus demand bilingual education and seek group rights, 'brown pride,' and restoration of 'brown dignity,' while rejecting assimilation and Western culture."[56]

While critics of bilingual education, on the one hand, reified the racialization of Latinidad, they also challenged the psychologically damaged racialized subject that provided the foundation for the institutionalization of bilingual education in educational bureaucracies, which had become the primary rationale for bilingual education offered by Latinx professionals. For example, journalist Glenn Garvin, in his description of the passage of the BEA, argued that "Hispanic activists flocked to testify for the bill, and very few of them said anything about learning English. Instead, they argued that the high dropout rate was due to the fact that Hispanic kids had low self-esteem because they weren't being taught in their native language."[57] He went on to trace the ways that this focus on self-esteem and the supposed cognitive damage of English-only instruction led to the creation of what he termed "facilitation theory," which suggested that students needed to fully develop literacy skills in their home language to prevent cognitive damage, and this would then allow them to transfer these skills into English. He argued that facilitation theory "gave a patina of intellectual respectability not only to bilingual education but to gringo bashing" and "further strengthened the entrenched bureaucracy of bilingual education that was more invested in protecting the livelihood of the Latinx professionals working in bilingual education as opposed to serving the best interest of Latinx students."[58] For Garvin, the vested interest in the educational bureaucracy in facilitation theory served to disempower Latinx students and their families by framing professionals as knowing better than parents and communities, an ideology that he succinctly described as "we know better, we're the teachers."[59] In this way, the doubling down on deficit perspectives required for gaining access to these educational bureaucracies was subsequently mobilized against them by bilingual education critics to call into question their political motives and frame them as militant out-of-touch ideologues imposing nonsensical theories on Latinx communities.

Banning Bilingual Education

The political assault on bilingual education culminated in its banning in California in 1998. A focal point of these efforts was a parent boycott of a downtown Los Angeles elementary school to protest the use of bilingual education in the school, organized by an Episcopalian priest named Alice Callaghan. Juana Losara, a Mexican mother participating in the boycott, described going to the school when she heard that her children were receiving less than an hour a day of English instruction and being told to be patient, an answer she rejected because of her belief that "if they don't learn English at this age, at 9 or 10, they aren't going to speak it when they grow up," which would not allow them to "be something" despite the many struggles and sacrifices she and her husband have made for them.[60] Many bilingual education activists suggested that Losara and the parents participating in the boycott were being manipulated by Callaghan. Yet, Losara rejected such claims, insisting, "it was our idea, we were the ones who wanted to do it."[61] Critics of bilingual education were able to connect this boycott with the broader discursive construction of bilingual education as an entrenched educational bureaucracy more invested in its own maintenance than in actually serving Latinx communities, who were now beginning to revolt against this bureaucracy.

One prominent critic who promoted this narrative was Silicone Valley millionaire Ron Unz, who used the parent boycott as a focal point in his campaign for Proposition 227, which sought to ban bilingual education in

California, arguing that "immigrant parents were forced to begin a public boycott after the school administration refused to allow their children to be taught in English."[62] Building on the existing critiques of bilingual education as an entrenched bureaucracy, Unz was able to position his campaign in support of Proposition 227 as one built on "the common sense of ordinary people—white and Latino, Democrat and Republican—against the timid political elites of all these groups, unwilling to challenge the special interests that benefited from a failed system."[63] He connected the rise of this political elite to the War on Poverty, which he argued was informed by an ideology that "radically changed the terms of the American social compact, replacing the emphasis on assimilation with an emphasis on ethnic difference"[64] by replacing the "American melting pot" with the "diversity model" that "allots to blacks and Latinos and Asians their own separatist institutions" that "contains the seeds of national dissolution."[65] Unz, therefore, depicted bilingual education as not just a self-interested bureaucracy, but as also posing an existential threat to the very fabric of US society—what he tellingly referred to in the title of this commentary as "the end of white America."

This message was successful; the initiative passed with 61% of the vote. Unz also successfully led efforts to pass a similar initiative in Arizona in 2000 and Massachusetts in 2002, before experiencing his first defeat in Colorado. One major reason for this defeat was a $3 million contribution to the opposition campaign made by another millionaire, whose daughter was attending a dual-language school.[66] Advocates for bilingual education used this money to pay for commercials that were condemned by Unz as playing on the racist sentiments of the white population of Colorado. He described one of the commercials as "intended to play on the unsubtle fears of white conservative voters, running visually-gripping ads featuring throbbing doomsday music while an announcer claims 'We know that Amendment 31 will knowingly force children who can barely speak English into regular classrooms, creating chaos and disrupting learning.' "[67] That is, once again bilingual education advocates doubled down on deficit perspectives of Latinx children and reified their racialization in order to defend bilingual education.

The Racial Limits of Bureaucratization

A major consequence of the institutionalization of the BEA was an increasing federal bureaucracy which, in turn, produced an increasing state and local bureaucracy dedicated to overseeing the implementation of bilingual education. As a result, by the end of the 1970s, many bilingual education advocates who had gained their political experience in the 1960s context of community-control struggles found themselves working in and with the educational bureaucracies that they once criticized. The political trade-off that they had to make in gaining access to these educational bureaucracies was conditional proximity to whiteness through accepting the psychologically damaged racialized subject that suggested that Latinx children had unique cultural and linguistic deficiencies that bilingual education was well positioned to fix. Unfortunately, these efforts to approximate whiteness did not fundamentally transform the racialized status of these Latinx professionals, with critics depicting the efforts of these professionals to center the experiences of Latinx children as existential threats to the integrity of US society. This being the case, it might be worth connecting back to the experiences of Juana Losara. Many bilingual education activists sought to position her as a dupe who was being manipulated by white people to support her own oppression. Yet, the basic assumption that undergirded the educational bureaucracy that positioned itself as purportedly knowing better than her was that her children, as well as other Latinx children, had unique psychological damage that warranted their need for bilingual education. Perhaps it was the Latinx professionals who accepted this logic—because they believed that their individual access to educational bureaucracies would permit them to fundamentally transform them for the better—who were the actual dupes who has been manipulated by white people to support their own oppression.

8
Demanding Bilingual Choices, Receiving Bilingual Scraps

By 1967, Kenneth Clark, one of the two social psychologists who had conducted the doll experiment that would provide the theoretical foundation for the psychologically damaged racialized subject that informed the *Brown* decision, had begun to question the wisdom of continuing to advocate for integration considering the little progress that had been made in the face of white opposition. While still seeing integration as being the end goal, he saw the emerging struggles for community control of schools as one way of more immediately ensuring that Black children received a high-quality education. He was particularly intrigued by the alternative school movement, a national movement that sought to develop community-oriented schools within urban school districts. He described alternative schools as "realistic, aggressive and viable competitors to the present school system," concluding that "truly effective competition strengthens rather than weakens that which deserves to survive."[1] Utilizing discourse that parallels the ways that charter schools would be described decades later, he suggested that

> with a strong, efficient and demonstrably excellent parallel system of public schools, organized and operating on a quasi-private level, and with quality control and professional accountability maintained and determined by Federal and State educational standards and supervision, it would be possible to bring back into public education a viability and dynamism which are now clearly missing.[2]

Bilingual education activists also saw promise in the alternative school movement. In the 1974 Bilingual Education Act congressional hearings, Mario Anglada, the executive director of Aspira, celebrated the success of Aspira of New York in opening the Creating Resources for Educational Opportunity (CREO) program, an alternative high school in New York

Becoming the System. Nelson Flores, Oxford University Press. © Oxford University Press 2024.
DOI: 10.1093/oso/9780197516812.003.0008

City that offered a bilingual curriculum "which included English, Spanish, math, science, history, art, music and physical education taught by bilingual Puerto Rican teachers."[3] He lamented the fact that the CREO program had lost federal funding after "an unbelievably successful two years," though he noted that "much of the knowledge gained through the CREO faculty will be incorporated into new programs to be established at Aspira's Educational Opportunity Center," including continued work at developing bilingual alternative schools.[4] He pointed to Aspira of Illinois as one example that was "running a highly successful Bilingual Alternative School" that offered "a full course of instruction in Spanish and English as first and second languages, general math, general science, history and Latin American studies."[5] Thirty years later, the Bill and Melinda Gates Foundation announced that it would be giving Aspira of Illinois a $900,000 grant to support the expansion of the charter school model that they had created in subsequent years, which included plans for them to become a charter management organization.[6] This model was also followed by other Aspira state affiliates that received both state and philanthropic funds to open charter and alternative schools, with the organization as a whole operating fourteen charter schools by 2020.[7]

In this chapter, I will examine the relationship between bilingual education and the politics of school choice in the post–Civil Rights era. I will examine the ways that initial efforts by bilingual education advocates to engage with the politics of school choice in the 1970s failed not only because of political realities that prevented the enactment of educational vouchers for private schools, but also because notions of the public that is ostensibly served by public schools continued to be overrepresented as white in ways that constrained the possibilities available to alternative public schools. I then examine the ways that the bipartisan consensus that emerged related to charter schools in the 1990s offered a new pathway for bilingual education advocates to use in working to create bilingual schools outside of the existing public school bureaucracy. I will illustrate the ways that charter school reform can be understood as the culmination of the post–Civil Rights era move away from state efforts at combating racial inequities through funding programs that sought to fix the supposed cultural and linguistic deficiencies of racialized communities toward market-based solutions focused on increasing parental choice, while continuing to leave the existing structural barriers confronting racialized communities intact.

From Community Control to Schools of Choice

With community control of schools experiencing a decisive defeat in New York City amidst huge teacher union resistance, advocates for community control began to look to alternative approaches for creating their vision of schools run by and for the community. One challenge that immediately arose was how to fund these alternative schools.[8] Initially, advocates relied on funding from the Ford Foundation and other philanthropic organizations that were sympathetic to community control of schools. Yet, by 1974, the Ford Foundation indicated that it was no longer planning to support these schools and suggested that government funds must be used for these schools to remain viable.[9] This was also the case with other philanthropic organizations that primarily saw their role as providing start-up funds for educational innovation, rather than indefinite funding of the daily operation of schools.[10] The scramble for funding led many proponents of community control of schools to begin to advocate for more stable government funding for private schools, alternative schools within the public school system, or schools created as hybrid public-private partnerships. Importantly, these various proposals were not necessarily framed in opposition to one another, with many proponents of community control seeing each of these various possibilities as an opening to create more culturally and linguistically affirming schools for racialized students while increasing parental and community participation and control via school choice. In this chapter, I examine efforts to experiment with voucher programs and to develop alternative schools within the context of efforts to offer bilingual education as a choice for Latinx families before examining the relationship between bilingual education and charter schools alongside the increasing hegemony of neoliberalism within debates related to education reform.

Community Control, Bilingual Education, and Educational Vouchers

One effort to bring school choice into US schools supported by community-control advocates was to offer government funds to private schools in the form of educational vouchers that would be given to parents to use to pay for tuition at private schools of their choosing. First proposed by economist Milton Friedman in 1955,[11] the idea received increasing attention in the 1960s within the context of growing critiques of urban school bureaucracies in conjunction with calls for community control of schools.[12] During the political controversy that erupted at Ocean Hill–Brownsville, Theodore Sizer, then the dean of the Harvard Graduate School of Education, suggested that such a voucher system might be able to fulfill the original goals of community-control advocates while eliminating the political unrest that served as a distraction from these goals. Characterizing this as a "more radical plan" that "would employ public money to create separate, private school systems for minorities," he suggested that "this approach would decentralize by persuasion rather than geography,"[13] replacing the "need for a common school" with an approach that would "recognize and honor responsible diversity."[14] In the context of the decline of community control in the 1970s, the prominent education activist Jonathan Kozol made a similar point in his lauding of efforts by Bill Owens, a Black man who sued the city of Boston, demanding tuition reimbursement after removing his children from the public school system and placing them in a parent-operated free school. Kozol described these efforts as "a revolutionary's version of the voucher system," concluding that "this was a very eloquent idea," leading him to wonder "if more people and more organizations could not do this also."[15]

In response to these demands, in 1970 the Office of Economic Opportunity (OEO) announced a plan to fund experimental voucher demonstration districts. Initially, several districts expressed interest, though while conducting OEO feasibility studies many decided not to pursue the project in the face of strong teacher union opposition that paralleled teacher union opposition to community control of schools. The only district that committed to pursuing the demonstration project was Alum Rock, a small K–8 school district of approximately 15,000 students across twenty-four schools in San Jose, California, with a large and growing Latinx student population.[16] Yet, the failure of the California legislature to pass legislation that would permit state funds to go to private schools put a significant roadblock to the implementation of the voucher demonstration. Because William Jefferds, the district superintendent, saw the voucher demonstration as a way of getting federal funds to support decentralization efforts that he had already begun implementing and the OEO was under congressional pressure to create a voucher demonstration or lose funding, they agreed on a "transition" voucher model that would offer parents choices among public schools, with the hope being that private schools might be incorporated in the future—a hope that never materialized.[17]

While the district was making moves toward adopting a voucher program, it was also beginning to experiment with bilingual education for its growing Latinx student population, with the first bilingual education program established in the same year that the district conducted its feasibility study.[18] The following year, while the district was making plans for implementing the voucher demonstration project, it launched Projecto Anglo-Latino at one of its elementary schools, which had the goal "to teach all children (of all ethnic backgrounds) English and Spanish in a bilingual-bicultural setting."[19] Yet for many bilingual education advocates, this was not enough. In particular, La Confederación de la Raza Unida pressured the district to implement more bilingual education programs as part of a more general call for more parent and student participation in decision-making emerging in 1972, the year of the voucher demonstration's office launch.[20] Joel Levin, the director of the Alum Rock Voucher Program, saw the voucher program as an opportunity to meet these demands because, as he noted:

> what is very critical about it, and perhaps controversial, is that the ultimate criteria as to whether a program will flourish or go down is not what an educator think abouts it, but what parents think about it. . . . All they have to do is to find parents who want their children in the program, and that decision will bring in the resources with which to carry on the program.[21]

For Levin, community control was still possible via parental choice, which in his view could pave the way to creating "a much more humane and responsive system,"[22] including through the harnessing of parental demand for "bilingual programs, which the district greatly needs."[23]

In 1972, Alum Rock created 22 mini-schools in 6 of its 24 schools, which expanded to 40 mini-schools in 13 schools in 1973, and 51 mini-schools in 14 schools in 1974. Each mini-school received a basic voucher worth the average per pupil cost for each family that selected their program, with an additional "compensatory" voucher for "disadvantaged children."[24] The largest number of mini-schools that opened were back-to-basics programs, with the second largest number of mini-schools being programs focused on individualization. Yet, in response to increasing demand from local community organizations, a sizable number of mini-schools were bilingual/bicultural, which were described as "programs focused on language arts in a culturally pluralistic context. Basic skills instruction was said to proceed in the students' first language (either Spanish or English), with considerable emphasis on learning a second language (English for Spanish-speaking students, and Spanish for English-speaking students)."[25] By the second year of implementation, Joel Levin reported that full-fledged bilingual mini-schools had emerged in response to parental demand.[26] In addition, there were reports that some of the mini-schools categorized as individualized were also experimenting with bilingual education, and the strategic use of Spanish was reported in some of these classrooms in the name of individualization.[27]

In 1974, momentum for the voucher demonstration began to wane, primarily because of the end of federal funding to support the project, coupled with district budget challenges resulting from declining enrollment and increasing district costs due to inflation. Teacher layoffs based on seniority, rather than on specific skills such as bilingualism or affinity to specific pedagogical approaches, made it increasingly difficult to sustain a coherent vision for the various mini-schools. In line with teacher layoffs were the fixing of class sizes across the mini-schools so that the district could accurately predict how many teachers they would need, meaning that mini-schools could no longer acquire more money by enrolling more students. This was the beginning of a recentralization process, with the mini-schools losing even more autonomy in the subsequent year of the project, culminating in the Alum Rock Board of Trustees voting to limit the number of mini-schools per building to three. By 1977, only two schools were offering mini-schools, effectively marking the end of the voucher demonstration project.[28] While bilingual education continued in Alum Rock, it would now continue via a centralized Bilingual Education Policy in a context of increasingly precarious funding[29] and was eventually banned in 1997 with the passage of Proposition 227 banning bilingual education across the state.

Community Control, Bilingual Education, and Alternative Schools

A more prominent effort to bring school choice into US schools was the development of alternative public schools that were given autonomy to create their own programming, which they could use to attract students and families who found their educational approach appealing. One prominent spokesperson for the creation of these alternative schools was Mario Fantini, the former Ford Foundation officer who oversaw the funding of community-control experiments in New York City and around the country. Making a direct link between his original liberal multicultural support for community control of schools in the 1960s and his strong support for these "public schools of choice" in the 1970s, he argued that

> the cry for community control of schools or, more accurately, the struggle that the minority groups and the poor are waging for self-determination in their schools, is in fact an expression of the need of the people of a community to participate in the fundamental decisions that affect their lives.[30]

In addition to solving the challenge of stable funding, Fantini suggested that public schools of choice met the original goals of community-control advocates by allowing for the development of a diversity of schooling options that would empower these disaffected communities by giving "the voice of the consumer more leverage," thereby developing a "get tough attitude toward professional domination" allowing for "new forms of accountability."[31] By 1975 there were 1,200 alternative schools across the nation,[32] including some that offered bilingual education.[33]

As was the case for educational vouchers, the federal government also allocated funding for alternative schools through the Experimental Schools Program (ESP) launched in 1970 by the US Office of Education. In 1971, ESP selected Berkeley, Minneapolis, and Tacoma to receive funding to support a five-year experiment in alternative education. Berkeley was an early experimenter with alternative schools, with the first school opening in 1967 as a "continuation" school for students expelled from the sole high school in the district.[34] By the time that it was selected to receive the grant, it already had nine alternative schools begun with funding received from philanthropic organizations.[35] Soon after receiving the grant, it had expanded the number to twenty-three. In contrast to Alum Rock, which had a relatively large and growing Latinx student population, Berkeley was about evenly divided between white and African American students (about 44% each) with only a 3% Latinx student population. Despite these relatively small numbers, one of the alternative schools the district opened using these federal funds was Casa de la Raza, which had the goal of creating educational programs that "are free from the white, middle-class biases and pressures allegedly characteristic of an ordinary school environment,"[36] with a specific focus on bilingual education.

Casa de la Raza connected to a broader Chicano alternative education movement that sought "to develop a viable alternative to conventional institutions that have historically failed to respond to the educational needs of Chicanos" because of "the inability of institutions to address the diverse interests and needs of the population and adopt a pluralist ethic."[37] Informed by the race radicalism that provided the foundation of many community-control struggles of the era, at the core of the Chicano alternative education movement was the concept of Chicanismo that sought to center the cultural and linguistic history of the Chicano community. The Chicano alternative education movement inspired a range of educational innovations, both in the K–12 schools and at the college level, supplemented by after-school and summer programs.[38] In the spirit of community-control struggles, and in line with a race radical vision, the goal was to create options for Chicano families and communities outside of the existing white power structure.

As an outgrowth of this broader movement, Casa de la Raza was organized around Chicanismo, which Francisco Hernandez, the principal, described as "stressing cooperation rather than competition . . . brotherhood rather than having dog-eat-dog."[39] For Hernandez, the enactment of Chicanismo could not come from "slight reform" but rather "basic redesign."[40] For Hernandez, such a redesign entailed hiring "a Chicano director and a Chicano assistant director, Chicano teachers," using "as many Chicano materials as possible" in "addressing Chicano problems with Chicano resolutions rather than trying to deal with Chicano problems in gabacho fashion."[41] He described bilingualism and biculturalism as playing an integral role in enacting Chicanismo and described the ways that the school had expanded the Spanish program as part of their efforts at "developing the bicultural aspect of the Chicano part of the children," reporting that "we did this through various means—from materials, through outside activities, through models played by our teachers."[42] He also reported soliciting funds to develop alternative assessments that reflected the principles of Chicanismo and would, therefore, be more valid indicators of the success of the school.[43] This model proved popular, with 125 of the district's 427 Chicano students reported to be attending the alternative school by its second year of operation.[44]

While the school was popular within the Chicano community, it, along with Black House that followed a similar model for African American students in Berkeley, proved to be politically controversial. A year after their opening, Arkansas Senator John L. McClellan wrote a letter to the Office of Civil Rights inquiring into why Berkeley's Experimental Program was permitted to operate racially segregated schools while Arkansas was being forced to desegregate. A legal argument made in response to these concerns was articulated by a law student named Susan Frelich Appleton. Adopting a liberal multicultural rationale, she described the schools as "remedial and corrective programs adopted to eliminate the frequently poor academic performance of black and Chicanos in ordinary educational environments, which are typically geared to the needs and interests of the white, middle-class pupil."[45] Framing it within the same psychologically damaged racialized subject that undergirded the case for school integration, she argued that "if Black House and Casa improve the self-confidence and academic achievement of their students more effectively than integrated schools, these schools would appear to fulfill a compelling state interest."[46] She argued that such an approach was similar to the philosophy of transitional bilingual education in that the goals of both are "to prepare a student for true equality in the context of subsequent integration, and remedial work plays a significant role in each," with the key difference being that while "bilingual education need only encompass a brief period in each student's career, it is arguable that the type of preparation Black House and Casa aim to provide simply requires a substantially longer period of time."[47] In short, her argument was that the schools were very much in line with the same ideological foundation of the *Brown* decision, as well as with subsequent efforts to institutionalize transitional bilingual education in that they were designed as compensatory education that would better support Black and Chicano students in assimilating into whiteness. This argument was endorsed by proponents of the Chicano alternative education movement who, while espousing more race radical sentiments, reproduced the same psychologically damaged racialized subject as part of their support for the school.[48]

The US government did not, however, find these arguments compelling. After an investigation, the Office of Civil Rights concluded that both schools were not in compliance with Title VII of the Civil Rights Act and ordered them to be closed. Many of the other alternative schools in the district also struggled, and most of the ones developed using federal funding were quickly phased out due to lack of enrollment. By the end of the decade, the alternative school movement had essentially disappeared from Berkeley, alongside any hopes for developing Chicano alternatives to white-controlled schooling that centered bilingual education.

Community Control, Bilingual Education, and Charter Schools

A third effort to bring school choice into US schools was through a hybrid public-private partnership in the form of contracted schools where school districts hired private organizations to manage district schools.[49] These ideas were synthesized by educator Ray Budde in a 1974 conference presentation at the Society for General Systems Research into an idea he referred to as "education by charter."[50] While there was little immediate uptake of this idea outside of a few small experiments, it would gradually gain support and would provide the ideological foundation for the first charter school law, passed in Minnesota in 1991, which quickly spread around the country.[51] By 1995, charter schools had achieved bipartisan consensus, with Bill Clinton challenging "every state to give all parents the right to choose which public school their children will attend and to let teachers form new schools with a charter they will keep only if they do a good job."[52]

Many participants in the alternative school movement saw parallels between this newly emerging charter school movement and their previous efforts to mobilize school choice as a way of enhancing parent and community control of schools. One district superintendent with extensive experience in the alternative school movement made direct parallels between the original vision of the alternative school movement and the newly emerging charter school movement, noting that in both, "professional staff enjoyed a great latitude in the delivery of instruction and in management. Course content was consistent with the school districts' adopted curriculum, but the emphasis was determined by the parents... [and] money was allocated to alternative schools from the districts' general fund typically on a per-student basis or using staff allocation as the determinant."[53] Indeed, though the concept of a charter school is attributed to educator Ray Budde, we can see traces of this idea in earlier struggles for community control of school, such as when a charter was signed between the Navajo community of Rough Rock and the Bureau of Indian Affairs in 1968 to allow the community to create a community-controlled school that would instruct students bilingually in Navajo and English and serve as a cultural hub for the entire community.[54] In line with this history, the National Alliance for Public Charter Schools documented 131 charter schools that reported some type of cultural focus that included ethnocentric, bilingual, and dual language immersion by 2012.[55]

Having made little traction with developing high-quality bilingual education programs, Aspira of Pennsylvania was offered a new pathway for enacting their vision with the passage of the Pennsylvania charter school law in 1997. It was one of the first organizations to take advantage of this law in 1998 when it opened Eugenio María de Hostos, a K–8 dual-language school in a Philadelphia neighborhood with a large and growing Latinx student population. In its first year of operation, the school sought to implement a high-quality bilingual and culturally relevant curriculum that Aspira of Pennsylvania had been advocating for, with little success, in the district for decades. Maria Quiñones-Sanchez, the executive director of Aspira of Pennsylvania, noted that "though a majority of the students are of Puerto Rican descent, most can't speak Spanish," adding that the school hoped "to reconnect them with that part of their heritage and to prepare the students for the multicultural world that awaits them courses are taught in English and Spanish on alternating weeks."[56] This bilingual aspect of the curriculum was complemented by a cultural aspect that sought to infuse Latinx history into the curriculum through, for example, the teaching of capoeira, a dance created by enslaved people in Brazil as a clandestine form of self-defense, or critical history lessons on the genocide that Christopher Columbus committed against Indigenous people. One student, Jose Colon, commented on the bilingual nature of the school, noting, "I like the school because we get to learn Spanish. And when I go to college, I'll know how to speak it."[57] In addition, the school created a parent council to ensure community involvement in ways that Aspira of Pennsylvania felt was lacking in the school district.[58]

Based on their success with Eugenio María de Hostos, in 2008 Aspira of Pennsylvania officially became a Charter Management Organization (CMO) to "work for quality education for students and meet parental demands for higher academic expectations in its neighborhood," with their rationale being that "charter schools have the flexibility to try inventive and creative ways of improving learning" and "give parents more options within the public school system, increasing their voice on educational quality expectations."[59] Utilizing similar discourse to that used by Kenneth Clark in the late 1960s, Aspira of Pennsylvania described this move toward charter schools as a "win-win for all students" in that these schools will exert "naturally increasing pressure on public school districts to achieve higher levels of educational excellence."[60] The same year, they opened Antonia Pantoja, another bilingual charter school, named after the founder of their organization, and opened a Bilingual Cyber Charter School two years later.[61]

Yet, 2008 was not 1968, and the proliferation of charter schools was occurring within the increasing hegemony of neoliberalism within education reform and in the broader society, which has inevitably shaped the debate over charter schools over the past two decades.[62] Whereas the Ford Foundation was the most prominent foundation funding these earlier initiatives, it was now the Broad Foundation and the Gates Foundation that were the most prominent organizations funding this agenda.[63] And whereas the earlier efforts of the Ford Foundation were connected to a liberal multicultural vision of educational reform that sought to promote racial equity by fixing the supposed cultural and linguistic deficiencies of racialized communities, these more recent efforts have been connected to a neoliberal vision of educational reform that seeks to promote racial equity through ensuring that everybody has the right to make their own choices in a marketplace assumed to be free and equal.[64] What connects both efforts are processes of politically incorporating a professional cadre of racialized leaders into the existing power structure in ways that divorce them from the daily struggles of their communities.

In the case of Philadelphia, this neoliberal reframing came most notably in the exponential growth in charter schools in the district since the passing of the Pennsylvania charter school law in 1997. By 2013, almost one-third of Philadelphia's district budget went to charter schools.[65] A related component of this neoliberalism was the bringing in of CMOs to manage districts schools that had been identified as low performing. In line with this approach, in 2010 the School District of Philadelphia announced the Renaissance Initiative that created two options for selected low-performing schools. The first option was for schools to become Promise Academies, which would undergo a school turnaround but remain under district management. The second option was for schools to become Renaissance Schools, whose turnaround process would be managed by a CMO. In total, eleven schools were targeted for the Renaissance Initiative, and Aspira of Pennsylvania, after several years of managing its own independent charter school, was chosen to manage Stetson Middle School by its School Advisory Council. The following year, in 2011, the School Advisory Council of Olney High School also selected Aspira of Pennsylvania to be its CMO when it was slated to become a Renaissance School.[66] That said, while both Stetson and Olney served large Latinx student populations, neither of the schools had a bilingual education program, and Aspira of Pennsylvania did not make any significant efforts to develop these programs, with their primary focus being on discipline and safety.[67]

Aspira of Pennsylvania had its first opportunity to delve into bilingual education within its management of district schools when the third round of schools selected for the Renaissance Initiative were announced in the spring of 2014. In contrast to the first two rounds of the Initiative, where schools were slated to be either a Promise Academy or a Renaissance School, in this round the School Advisory Council would have the opportunity to choose which model they preferred, though they would no longer have a choice over which CMO would be selected to manage their school as an alternative to the district. One school selected for turnaround was Luis Muñoz-Marín, which at the time was the only district school in the city to be piloting a new dual-language education program. The CMO that was offered as an alternative to becoming a Promise Academy was Aspira of Pennsylvania. This process quickly became extremely contentious, with both Aspira of Pennsylvania and those who wanted the school to become a Promise Academy claiming that the other side was working to sabotage the process to prevent a fair selection process.[68]

Executive Director Alfredo Calderon made the case for why Aspira of Pennsylvania was well suited to manage Muñoz-Marín, arguing that the organization has "been supporting this community for 45 years," adding that "this is part of what we do, who we are. We live and work in this community."[69] In contrast to the current staff and programming at Luis Muñoz-Marín, he noted that in Aspira-managed schools "our teachers are younger. Our scores are higher . . . our trend is going up . . . their trend is going down."[70] In line with this, during Aspira of Pennsylvania's presentation to the school community, they shared performance growth data from Stetson and Olney, with a specific focus on success that they had with increasing the academic performance of special education students. Aspira of Pennsylvania's adoption of a neoliberal framework that relied on traditional accountability metrics in determining which schools were failing, and should, therefore, be managed by outside organizations, marks a significant shift from Casa de la Raza and other such schools that emerged in the early days of the alternative school movement that sought to challenge traditional accountability metrics because of their unexamined whiteness.

Muñoz-Marín teachers, supported by the Philadelphia Federation of Teachers (PFT), aligned themselves with parent leaders at the school to create a strong counteroffensive to Aspira of Pennsylvania. Yet, this counteroffensive didn't call into question the accountability metrics that Aspira presented; instead, they argued that their low performance was because they served students with higher needs than charter schools and had fewer resources to meet those needs. As parent Evelyn Sostre put it, Muñoz-Marín "has a high population of students with disabilities. Charter schools don't want half of the kids that we have because they already got rid of them. The ones the charter schools have not accepted. They're here." She concluded, "instead of going to charter schools and giving them all of the extra money put it back into the public school system and let them succeed."[71] In this way, both sides accepted the basic premise that the goal of public education is to help racialized students assimilate into whiteness, with the relevant question being whether this can be best done under district management or by a private organization, and what the necessary resources were to ensure that this successfully occurred.

Parents overwhelmingly voted to remain under district management. Yet, it was a hollow victory, with more than half of the teachers having already requested transfers before the final decision had been made because of the uncertainty. This included many of the bilingual teachers who had been teaching in the pilot dual-language program. In the following year, one of the bilingual teachers reported to me that the lack of bilingual teachers to teach in the program resulted in the first cohort of students being transitioned into mainstream classrooms, with the program essentially starting again from scratch. She also reported that many mandates of the district-managed turnaround made it difficult to implement the dual-language program with fidelity, undermining the hard work that they had undertaken to raise the status of bilingualism at the school. It seemed to me like the history of Potter-Thomas, described in Chapter 1, repeating itself once again. The key difference is that new sides had been drawn, with Aspira of Pennsylvania and Muñoz-Marín teachers and parents fighting over who can most effectively manage the assimilation of the predominantly Latinx students attending the school into whiteness. Both sides were fighting for scraps in a system that was designed to maintain the racial status quo—and, in this way, they both lost before the fight even began.

9

Selling Bilingual Education, Inheriting Racial Inequality

In the 1970 Georgetown University Round Table of Languages and Linguistics, prominent bilingual education scholar Joshua Fishman made the case for making bilingual education available for all children in the United States:

> The day is coming when more and more genuine bilingual education, for all those who want it, regardless of income, mother tongue or language dominance, will be part of the variegated picture of American education. At this time it will not be a mere euphemism for programs in English as a second language which, though unquestionably essential, constitute only one part and one kind of dual language education. It will not be just a promissory note to the poor, nor a left handed contribution to increasingly vocal and organized (though still exploited and dispossessed) Hispanos and Indians. It will be available to my children and grandchildren, and to yours, because it's too good to keep it from all the people.[1]

Fishman was writing at a time where bilingual education was typically seen as compensatory education focused on meeting the needs of students identified as having sufficiently limited English to justify their participation in such a program. The idea that bilingual education could be a program that was not compensatory, but rather an option for all, may have seemed naively idealistic to many of his contemporaries. Yet, fifty years later, it would seem like Fishman's vision is closer to becoming a reality than ever before, with the exponential growth in the number of dual-language programs across the country, open to students of all linguistic backgrounds,[2] coupled with the passing of the seal of biliteracy that offers a seal on the diplomas of high school graduates demonstrating the ability to read and write in a language other than English in all 50 states and DC.[3] While these developments have typically been applauded by bilingual education advocates, a more critical

Becoming the System. Nelson Flores, Oxford University Press. © Oxford University Press 2024.
DOI: 10.1093/oso/9780197516812.003.0009

examination of this shift in favor of bilingualism for all indicates some troublesome power dynamics that have emerged related to race, language, and social class.

This dynamic can be illustrated by the opening of a new dual-language program in Holyoke, Massachusetts, in 2014. According to Anna Lugo, the English Language Learners director for the district, the impetus for starting the program was a dual-language exploratory preschool program that attracted "a lot of monolingual English parents who wanted their children to get the second language experience" and whom the district struggled to keep in the school after entering kindergarten.[4] Making the case for a dual-language program as a way to sell the schools to these parents, she argues, "if you tell an English speaking family that their children can be bilingual in four years at no additional cost to them, it's a very exciting opportunity."[5] By 2019, the school had moved from having a dual-language program to becoming a dual-language school with a waiting list for enrollment. In describing the school, Principal Amy Burke noted, "We have kids who have never spoken a lick of Spanish going home and speaking Spanish."[6] Dual-language teacher Militza Semiedi described the benefits of the program by suggesting, "if you want to learn another language you have to go abroad and do an exchange or visit and immerse yourself in that culture. Here you don't have to do that because the students are getting the first-hand experience."[7] That is, in their efforts to create the opportunity for bilingualism for all, in the ways that Fishman envisioned, these educators focused their primary attention for justifying these programs on the purported benefits that these programs offer to affluent monolingual white families who would otherwise send their children to private school and/or to study-abroad experiences to learn Spanish.

This dynamic of privileging the needs and desires of affluent monolingual white families is further illustrated by tensions that erupted at Tyler Elementary School, a predominantly African American school in Washington, DC, in 2018, related to the possible growth of its existing dual-language program and the phasing out of its general education program. The dual-language program had a 34% white student population, while the rest of the school had only a 7% white student population. Kristin Pugh, an African American mother of a child at Tyler Elementary, was skeptical of efforts to expand the program, arguing, "you are trying to push out the minority," adding that "it's happening all over the city."[8] These sentiments were shared by Carla Norde, another African American mother, who argued, "the more white parents that get involved in the school, they are the ones pushing these agendas. We have always been in that school, and we have never been pushing that agenda."[9] Here we have predominantly white parents working to fulfill Fishman's dream of ensuring bilingual education for all families at the school their children attended pitted against the long-standing African American community who felt like their needs and desires were being placed to the side as part of their systematic displacement from the gentrifying community where they have resided for generations.

Both anecdotes point to a discursive shift in how bilingual education is being framed. Within the context of the institutionalization of bilingual education in the post–Civil Rights era, bilingual education was primarily situated within a liberal multicultural framing that positioned it as part of a broader effort to fix the supposed linguistic and cultural deficiencies of Latinx communities. Since the banning of bilingual education in California in 1998, there has been a gradual discursive shift toward a neoliberal multicultural framing that positions bilingual education as a commodity that increasingly caters to affluent monolingual white families.[10] In this chapter, I examine the ascendency of neoliberal multiculturalism, with a particular focus on the ways that the emergence of this discursive formation has connected to discursive shifts in bilingual education since the dawn of the 21st century.

Neoliberal Multiculturalism, Converse Racialization, and Bilingual Education

At the core of both liberal and neoliberal multiculturalism is a conceptualization of racial equity that provides tentative access to mainstream institutions for a subset of racialized people who are adopt behaviors that seek to approximate whiteness. In the case of liberal multiculturalism, these efforts to approximate whiteness come in the form of accepting the racialized perspective that the cultural and linguistic deficiencies of their communities are the root of their inability to achieve social mobility, and the solution is to fix them. In contrast, neoliberal multiculturalism is produced through discourses of converse racialization that remove these racialized cultural and linguistic practices from their communities and reframe them as unmarked mobile resources for the consumption of affluent white people.[11] Within this discursive formation, racialized people are able to approximate whiteness through successfully commodifying their "diversity" in ways that maintain global capitalism and obscure the continued legacy of white settler colonialism and anti-Blackness in shaping the institutions now clamoring for more diversity and inclusion within their walls.[12]

The failure of liberal multicultural defenses in preventing the banning of bilingual education in California, Arizona, and Massachusetts paved the way for the emergence of a neoliberal multicultural justification that shifted the discourse away from "bilingual education" for "limited-English-proficient students" to "dual-language education for all."[13] The resulting exponential growth in dual-language education helped to build momentum for the repeal of these bilingual education bans. This began with the repeal of Proposition 227 via Proposition 58 in California in 2016, which passed in a landslide with 73% of the vote. What changed from 1998, when Proposition 227 was passed, to 2016, when Proposition 58 repealed it, was the increasing prevalence of neoliberal multiculturalism that reappropriated discourses related to the Civil Rights movement in ways that, through converse racialization, separated these discourses from broader political struggles in favor of superficial celebrations of diversity.[14] In the following, I examine the converse racialization at play in Proposition 58, passed in California in 2016, illustrating the ways that it once again reconfigures bilingual education in ways that maintain existing racial inequities.

Neoliberal Multiculturalism, Converse Racialization and Proposition 58

At the core of Proposition 58 is the framing of the linguistic diversity of California as an asset, with the state being described as "a natural reserve of the world's largest languages."[15] The Proposition argues that these languages, in particular "English, Mandarin, and Spanish," are "critical to the state's economic trade and diplomatic efforts."[16] The Proposition argues that multilingualism is necessary for filling the needs of "multinational businesses that must communicate daily with associates around the world."[17] Specifically, the Proposition argues that California employers "are actively recruiting multilingual employees because of their ability to forge stronger bonds with customers, clients, and business partners."[18] Therefore, bilingual education is framed throughout the Proposition as primarily a tool for more effectively preparing *all* students for their role in the contemporary neoliberal political economy through being productive workers.

In line with its neoliberal framing, Proposition 58 frames the lack of quality choices as the primary barrier confronting *all* parents. From this perspective, the solution becomes to offer more choices, with bilingual education being one choice that parents would have available to them. Specifically, Proposition 58 makes the case for the importance of offering parents "a choice and voice to demand the best education for their children."[19] In particular, it argues that "parents now have the opportunity to participate in building innovative new programs that will offer pupils greater opportunities to acquire 21st century skills,"[20] with multilingualism being one such skill. In this vein, the Proposition argues that parents should have the choice to have "their children educated to high standards in English and one or more additional languages . . . thereby increasing pupils' access to higher education and careers of their choice."[21] The Proposition asserts that allowing parents to choose language programs "will improve their children's preparation for college and careers and allow them to be more competitive in a global economy."[22]

For Proposition 58, the argument is that providing *all* parents with the option of high-quality bilingual education will meet the needs of immigrant communities while providing much needed language skills for monolingual (white) communities. While on one level, this neoliberal multicultural discourse seems more progressive than liberal multicultural framings of the purported cultural and linguistic deficiencies of Latinx communities as being the primary rationale for bilingual education, it continues to obscure the structural barriers confronting Latinx and other racialized communities through an assumption that these communities are on a level playing field with the white middle-class families that these rebranded bilingual programs are seeking to attract. It also engages in converse racialization that leaves unaddressed the intense policing of the language practices of racialized communities and the normalization of identical language practices within white communities. Most relevant to the argument of this book, it works from the assumption that the bilingualism of both Latinx and white students will be equally valued, even though mainstream representations of Latinx bilingualism continue to be racialized through discourses with direct origins in the culture of poverty that connect to broader colonial histories.[23]

In summary, Proposition 58 relies on the neoliberal multicultural framing of bilingualism as a commodity that should be available to all communities. While embracing this neoliberal multiculturalism may offer a politically expedient way of countering attacks on bilingual education, it does so in ways that leaves white supremacy intact. At best, Latinx students become commodities who can be exploited by white middle-class families to further improve the economic prospects of their already privileged children.[24] At worst, because of the entrenched racism of US schools and the broader society, they may be systematically excluded from these programs as they refocus their attention to the interests of affluent white communities.[25] It is this disavowal of the root causes of racialization through discursive processes of converse racialization, which extract racialized bilingualism from Latinx communities and convert it into a lucrative commodity for affluent white people. This maintains the white supremacist logic that places the onus on racialized communities to undo their own oppression, a continuation of the logic that shaped liberal multicultural approaches to bilingual education.

Philadelphia and the Limits of Converse Racialization

In the previous section, I examined the converse racialization embedded within the discursive formation at the core of Proposition 58. In this section, I use my own collaboration on the effort to expand dual-language education in Philadelphia as a point of entry for examining the limits of such converse racialization in impacting the discursive terrain surrounding dual-language education within contexts of intense racialized poverty. In 2013, the School District of Philadelphia announced a new effort to expand dual-language education. At the time the district had four English-Spanish transitional bilingual education programs and one pilot dual-language program at Luis Muñoz-Marín. District leaders expressed a range of rationales for this move away from transitional to dual-language education. On the one hand, district officials were concerned with the academic performance of students officially classified as English language learners and pointed to research that indicated that these students academically performed better in dual-language than in transitional bilingual or ESL programs. On the other hand, they saw the expansion of dual-language education as a way of competing with the four dual-language charter schools in existence at the time, as well as a possible avenue for increasing student enrollment by attracting affluent white parents back into the public school system. In this way, district leaders sought to honor the original goal of bilingual education in meeting the needs of students deemed limited enough in English to warrant special language services, while breaking out of the remedial framing that provided the foundation of these policies by offering the program as a high-quality choice for all families. In the following, I examine case studies of two of the schools that were part of this initiative to offer a further illustration of the limits of the neoliberal multicultural framing of bilingual education reflected in initiatives such as Proposition 58 and others that have emerged around the country.[26]

Washington Elementary School

Washington Elementary School is a K–8 school located in a racially and linguistically diverse and gentrifying area of Philadelphia.[27] A new principal with a strong ESL background arrived at the school in 2013 amidst declining student enrollment within a context of district-led school closures of schools experiencing similar declines. One student population that was growing were students from Spanish-speaking backgrounds as a result of an influx of Mexican immigrants to the area over the past several years. The convergence of this growing Mexican immigrant population, a desire to attract more affluent white parents moving into the neighborhood as part of broader efforts to expand student enrollment, and the new district-wide initiative focused on expanding dual-language education programs announced at the end of the 2013 school year led to growing momentum for the creation of a dual-language program at the school beginning in the 2014–2015 school year.

You may recall Washington Elementary as the school where the mother mentioned in Chapter 1 asked me for advice on raising her children trilingual in English with her, Spanish via the dual-language program at the school, and Mandarin via their Mandarin-speaking nanny. As news got out about the program, more and more affluent white parents with similar desires and goals began clamoring to get their children into the program based on converse racialization that framed Spanish not as a language used by their neighbors, but as a commodity with supposed cognitive benefits that would bring better job prospects for their children in the global economy. This converse racialization, which framed the program as the "best fit" for their child, with little substantive political commitments to racial equity, eventually culminated in a mass exodus of affluent white families from the first cohort of the program in favor of special-admit middle schools when the students reached the fifth grade.

The year following this mass exodus, the principal invited me to the school to present to the fourth-grade parents about the benefits of dual-language education in the hopes of preventing another mass exodus. One parent argued that her child had already learned Spanish and that she was no longer being challenged in the program. When I suggested the possibility of language loss without sustained practice, she countered that she could hire her child a Spanish tutor to continue practicing her Spanish while attending a special-admit middle school that was the "best fit" for preparing her for admission to a special-admit high school. At the end of the meeting, the dual-language coordinator made an appeal to the group, arguing that the Spanish-speaking students in the program had provided language models for their children to learn Spanish, and that now that the program was moving into half of their instruction in English, they had the ethical obligation to allow their children to be the language models. The room remained awkwardly silent.

During that silence, I couldn't help but think of the many low-income Latinx children at the school whose families would have benefited from their participation in the program but who were turned away because there were no longer any slots for "Spanish-dominant" students. I began to think about the many other multilingual students at the school who may have thrived in learning Spanish since they were already multilingual. I thought about how these students were denied entry to the program in order to make space for affluent white families who brought desperately needed political power and resources to the school, but who were unreliable and inconsistent in sharing their power and resources with the other students in the dual-language program, let alone the entire school. I thought about all of that—and felt completely powerless to do anything to change that dynamic.

Hamilton Elementary School

In contrast to Washington Elementary school, Hamilton Elementary School[28] is a K–4 school in the same high-poverty, predominantly Latinx neighborhood as both Potter-Thomas and Luis Muñoz-Marín. While the new dual-language program began the same year as Washington Elementary School's, the principal was not enthusiastic and treated it mostly as a district mandate. A new Puerto Rican principal replaced her the following year and was much more enthusiastic about the program, based on her own extensive experience in bilingual education. A new staff person at the district offices who was familiar with Washington Elementary School and had worked in similar dual-language programs in gentrifying neighborhoods saw the renewed energy as an opportunity to replicate Washington's model by marketing the dual-language program through converse racialization that framed Spanish as a commodity that would be appealing to white families. I expressed skepticism that the school would be able to attract affluent white families because of its location in what some refer to as the "Badlands," an area of the city that has experienced institutional neglect, resulting in multiple generations of racialized poverty and the resulting violence typically associated with such poverty.[29] I even shared with her my experience at the parent meeting discussed in Chapter 1 where a Puerto Rican mother came to see if a dual-language program could support her child in overcoming the trauma of their homelessness. I suggested that the focus should be on ensuring high-quality dual-language education for the existing community served by the school, rather than to try to market the program to families who would likely not come. The district official initially pushed back on my suggestion, insisting that if the program were strong enough that affluent white parents clamoring for more options for their children would flock to it. After visiting the school, she conceded the point that the massive poverty of the surrounding neighborhood would make it impossible to market the school in the ways that she had envisioned and that she now agreed that it made sense to focus on making it effective for the existing student population. She came to realize that the community context was simply too racialized for converse racialization to be a viable option for attracting affluent white families.

My research team, along with district officials, had preliminary meetings with the newly hired bilingual teachers that the principal had recruited to the school. The energy was high at these meetings, with the principal insisting that she wanted the program to become a model for the other schools in the neighborhood that served a similar student population. Yet, she quickly experienced resistance from the majority white teaching staff at the school who accused her of favoring the new bilingual teachers, with some suggesting that it was because they were all Puerto Rican. Indeed, even some of the bilingual teachers who had been there before her arrival suggested that the move from a transitional bilingual education model to a dual-language education model was not a "good fit" for their student population since it was an enrichment model more appropriate for affluent white children. This massive resistance began to suck the momentum out of the implementation of the program.

Momentum decreased even more based on the many logistical problems that were beyond the control of the teachers and even the principal. As had been the case with Potter-Thomas over the years it implemented a bilingual education program, a particularly salient challenge was the high rate of student mobility, with students entering and leaving the school regularly as a result of the many instabilities of living in racialized poverty. While getting new students throughout the year is challenging in any classroom, there are unique challenges for dual-language classrooms. For example, teachers would sometimes get students with little to no experience with Spanish but would still be expected to instruct half of the day in Spanish—and to do so with little to no support. While there are certainly many pedagogically sound reasons for not placing students into dual-language education midyear, especially when they have had little to no experience with Spanish, the situation was not as clear-cut to the principal. The district policy of teacher allocation assigned one teacher for every 30 students in K–3, and one teacher for every 33 students in Grade 4, making it difficult for her to justify smaller classes for the dual-language program, especially when confronted with teachers who were already skeptical of her enthusiasm for the program. As a result, she often felt like she had no choice but to put students into dual-language classrooms during the middle of the year. She and I had many candid conversations about the constraints that she confronted, and I felt ill-equipped to provide her with concrete guidance on how best to proceed. Instead, what I came to realize was the unreasonable expectation that had been put on the dual-language program to magically increase the academic performance of students in the face of seemingly insurmountable structural barriers, many of which were beyond the control of anybody in the school.

The Anti-Racist Limits of Neoliberal Multiculturalism

With repeals of bans on bilingual education and the exponential increase in the number of dual-language programs, it appears that bilingual education is more widely accepted now than it has ever been since its re-emergence as a policy within the context of the War on Poverty. Indeed, once prominent assaults on bilingual education have seemingly become a footnote in the history of bilingual education, with people now describing English-only laws in education as "on verge of extinction."[30] Yet, a closer look at the contemporary discursive terrain reveals the convergence of discourses promoting bilingual education and the broader discursive formation of neoliberal multiculturalism. As with this broader discursive formation, at the core of the recent spread of dual-language education has been converse racialization, which extracts bilingualism from local communities and reframes it as a disembodied commodity that should be available to "everybody." As revealed throughout this chapter, because "everybody" has been overrepresented as white, this leads to centering the needs of white communities while erasing the racialization of Latinxs and other communities.[31]

Yet this is not just about the racialization of Latinxs. Instead, the commodification of language that provides the root of this converse racialization is produced in relation to white settler colonialism and anti-Blackness. Notably, Native American languages are often excluded from neoliberal multicultural framings of bilingual education, with the assumption being that these languages will not support increased competitiveness in the global economy. This can be seen with the status of Navajo in the widely celebrated Utah dual-language initiative. While appearing in early discussions related to the expansion of dual-language programs in the state, it quickly disappeared from the discourse as neoliberal multicultural framings of the programs increasingly dominated the debate.[32] In addition to the displacement of African American communities that is being exacerbated by the proliferation of dual-language programs in cities like Washington, DC, persistent raciolinguistic ideologies frame African Americans as verbally deprived and, therefore, not suitable for placement in dual-language programs.[33] In this way, while neoliberal multiculturalism purports to be promoting racial equity—and may even use terms like "anti-racism"—the reality is that it is the newest reconfiguration of white supremacy designed to reinforce the racial status quo.

I imagine some readers feeling frustrated by this analysis. One objection might be that the political realities of the moment necessitate bilingual education activists to strategically align themselves with neoliberal multicultural discourses to create bilingual spaces that can continue to serve Latinx students. Even if one accepts this argument, it is still important to critically interrogate the ways that this discourse is complicit in the continued reproduction of white supremacy. Failure to do so moves this from a strategic move toward one that simply reproduces and reifies the racial status quo. Some readers may even feel criticized by this analysis, having themselves relied on these discourses in their own advocacy work. But the analysis I have undertaken in this chapter is a structural one, not an individual one. It is about the limits of existing structures and not the ways that bilingual education activists navigate these fundamentally flawed structures. Indeed, I too have sometimes found myself working to strategically use neoliberal multiculturalism toward anti-racist goals, as I have discussed in this chapter. It is through my own work that I have come to see the limits of neoliberal multiculturalism. I have come to the conclusion that we can never commodify our way out of racial oppression, and the more that we try, the less we are bringing attention to the root causes of racial oppression.

10

A Raciolinguistic Genealogy of the Self

The original title for this final chapter was "Reclaiming a Race Radical Vision of Bilingual Education." I was hoping to build on previous arguments that I had made, related to how the original race radical vision of bilingual education was co-opted by liberal multiculturalism in ways that removed bilingual education from broader political struggles by reframing it as fixing the supposed linguistic and cultural deficiencies of Latinx students.[1] Yet as I engaged in the analysis for the book, I came to realize that the distinction between liberal multiculturalism and race radicalism was not as stark as I had originally believed, with both circulating at the emergence of bilingual education as a policy option in the mid-1960s and sometimes even used by the same individuals. I came to realize that this more complicated interrelationship was made possible by the fact that at the core of both liberal multiculturalism and race radicalism was the image of a psychologically damaged racialized subject, produced by either socialization into a maladaptive culture of poverty (in the case of liberal multiculturalism) or the pernicious effects of colonialism (in the case of race radicalism). This is not something that I want to reclaim, nor do I think that strategically using it for political mobilization will have anti-racist and decolonial outcomes. Framing racialized communities as damaged and in need of fixing will continue to harm these communities no matter how much we emphasize that it is structural rather than individual factors that have created this damage.

One solution to such a dilemma is to create new discourses that are not wedded to these colonial logics. This may be easier said than done since colonial logics shape the foundation of the institutions we are socialized into from birth. Yet, the power of genealogical thinking is the recognition that these efforts at interpellation are never completely determined and that it is in the excesses that cannot be fully contained where subversive practices can and do emerge.[2] In this spirit, inspired by calls for educators to engage in archaeologies of the self that critically reflect on how one's own life experience in relation to race impacts their pedagogy,[3] I have decided in this chapter to engage in a raciolinguistic genealogy of the self that situates my

Becoming the System. Nelson Flores, Oxford University Press. © Oxford University Press 2024.
DOI: 10.1093/oso/9780197516812.003.0010

professional trajectory in relation to the processes that I have examined in this book. Doing so allows me to reflect on the ways that my professional trajectory has been made possible as part of the reconfiguration of race in the post–Civil Rights era and the racializing discourses that were part of the institutionalization of bilingual education. I hope that implicating myself in this way serves to illustrate that my objective in writing this book was not to tear anybody down, but rather to use genealogical thinking to critically reflect on my own role as a Latinx professional working within bilingual education in the contemporary world.

Yet, the goal of implicating myself isn't to simply throw my hands up and say that whatever I do will inherently maintain colonial logics. Instead, I work to connect my own efforts to challenge these colonial logics throughout my professional career with the efforts of the previous generation of scholars and activists in the hopes of further teasing out the alternative worlds that have previously existed and continue to persist within the realm of academic knowledge production, which can be used to inspire a contemporary decolonial approach to bilingual education that colleagues and I have been working toward in recent years.[4] It should be noted that as an academic my focus in this chapter is specifically on academic knowledge production because this is where I can have the most immediate impact in (re)shaping the discourse. That said, I believe raciolinguistic genealogy of the self also has implications for policymakers and practitioners; it can support them in critically reflecting on their complicity in reproducing long-standing colonial logics, while also identifying the alternative worlds that already exist, which they can more effectively work to strengthen within their locus of control.

The Modern/Colonial Geopolitics of My Existence

A raciolinguistic genealogy of myself is situated within the white settler colonialism and trans-Atlantic slave trade that produced the Americas and subsequently Latin America. As Spanish colonizers created a permanent Creole class in the colonies, their claim to Europeanness came into question even as they and their European rulers continued to frame Black and Indigenous populations as not fully human and sought to eradicate their languages and replace them with Spanish. This shifting geopolitics between Spanish colonies and Spain, coupled with the rise of the United States as an imperial power, prompted Creoles to mobilize the image of "Latin people" with direct European lineage as a way of claiming their full Europeanness and of positioning themselves as leaders in shaping the future of the Americas. In this way, their vision of becoming modern continued colonial logics that disavowed the full humanity of Black and Indigenous people, in the hopes of gaining full status as Europeans for "Latin people" residing in "Latin America."[5]

Yet these efforts did little to change the emerging dynamics between the United States and Latin America, with US imperialism part of the geopolitical restructuring of the region, first as part of the Third World within the context of Cold War politics, and more recently as part of the Global South within the context of neoliberal globalization. An early manifestation of this imperial relationship was the US colonization of what would become the American Southwest after their victory in the Mexican–American War. Here a new racial order was mapped onto the existing white settler colonial racial order, with Creoles now becoming part of a broader group of Mexican Americans who were now a colonized group with precarious rights. In contrast to African Americans, whose racialization was developed via the "one drop rule" that argued that any "Black blood" constituted Black legal status regardless of one's phenotype, Mexican American racialization was developed via the "reverse one-drop rule" that argued that any "Spanish blood" constituted white legal status regardless of one's phenotype.[6] While this access to whiteness provided certain legal rights, it was also used to justify the continued oppression of Mexican Americans by denying them the right to make claims under the equal protection clause in the face of systemic discrimination across societal contexts including labor, education, and housing.[7] Here, the Spanish language, which in Latin America was colonially imposed on Black and Indigenous populations, became a mechanism for racializing Mexican Americans based on the assumption that the presence of Spanish in their communities justified their segregation in schools and their marginalization within the broader society.[8] As had been the case for Black and Indigenous languages throughout the Americas, Spanish now became a racialized language used to justify the oppression of Latinx communities residing in the United States.

A second significant event in cementing the imperial relationship between the United States and Latin America was the US colonial incorporation of Puerto Rico after their victory in the Spanish–American War. Like with the American Southwest, Puerto Rico had its own existing racial hierarchies, created through white settler colonialism, with the addition of enslaved

Africans brought to the island through the trans-Atlantic slave trade. As was also the case with the American Southwest, a new racialized category was created that framed all Puerto Ricans as on the one hand partially European, but on the other hand culturally, linguistically, and racially inferior. The goal, therefore, became to Americanize Puerto Ricans by offering them bilingual education that would provide them access to the English-speaking world, even as they were still denied equal political participation within US society or the right to self-determination because of a sense that their inferiorities made them incapable of self-governance. In this way, bilingual education was part of broader efforts to mold Puerto Ricans into becoming obedient laborers who accepted their inferior status within the US empire.[9] This colonial process continued in the post–World War II era with the implementation of Operation Bootstrap, which led to massive migration from rural to urban areas and an eventual mass migration from the island to the mainland, just as the agricultural and factory jobs that people were going in search of were on the decline—an economic modernization program that would become a model for the rest of Latin America and other parts of the Third World.[10]

As noted in previous chapters, Mexican Americans and Puerto Ricans became more directly linked with one another and with African Americans and Native Americans within the context of the culture of poverty discourse that rose to prominence in social science research in the 1950s. A major focus of this book has been the role of language in shaping the ideological foundation of this culture of poverty through verbal deprivation theory. In efforts to remediate this supposed verbal deprivation, African Americans received remediation solely through standardized forms of English, with the argument being that they had no additional legitimate language that could be incorporated.[11] Most Native Americans also received remediation through standardized forms of English, with the argument being that Native American languages did not have a sufficient literary tradition to be incorporated into educational interventions, with a few exceptions, most notably Navajo.[12] In contrast, Mexican Americans and Puerto Ricans were framed as having an additional legitimate language with a sufficient literary tradition to receive remediation through standardized forms of both English and Spanish. Yet, the incorporation of Spanish should not be interpreted as somehow valuing the home-language practices that Mexican American and Puerto Rican students brought into the classroom. On the contrary, their Spanish-language abilities were also interpreted through verbal deprivation theory such that they were framed as semilingual rather than bilingual.[13]

It was within this broader context that my family's story begins in the United States. My mother arrived to New York City from Puerto Rico when she was 12 years old as part of the massive migration from the island during Operation Bootstrap, described above. She arrived in 1962 just as the culture of poverty discourse was ascending into prominence within mainstream social science research. No doubt this culture of poverty discourse was part of why the Catholic school that she attended decided to place her in fourth grade rather than sixth grade, which is the grade she would have been entering had she stayed in Puerto Rico. It was also a time when bilingual education was just emerging as a policy option. As a result, her education upon arrival in the United States was officially English-only. Yet, many of her bilingual classmates would provide her support by translating for her—a role that she would eventually take on with the many Puerto Rican children who would come after her. She also had one kind bilingual nun who allowed her to compete in a multiplication table competition using Spanish, which allowed her to win. However, this was the exception that proved the rule, with bilingual education not being officially supported by the federal government until she was about to graduate from high school.

While Puerto Rico has experienced direct colonization by the United States, Ecuador has experienced US imperialism in more indirect ways. In 1951, the year my father was born, bananas were the country's biggest export—a policy decision that had been made in response to the increasing demand from the United States. Continuing the feudal system that had been enacted at the beginning of the white settler colonialism that provided the foundation for the nation, most of the lands used to harvest these bananas were owned by large, wealthy landowners, with most of the people harvesting the land giving a large part of their crops to these landowners in exchange for access to a small plot of land. As part of the expanding US imperialism in the region, the bulk of the profits from the actual exporting of the bananas were made by United Fruit and Standard Fruit, two US-based corporations. Such concentrated wealth, coupled with such heavy reliance on one crop, placed the country in an economically precarious position. This became increasingly apparent when disease began to affect banana crops, leading to massive unemployment by the 1960s and political instability throughout the decade.[14] One area that was particularly hard hit by this economic decline was Cañar Province, leading my father to decide to migrate to the United States, as the eldest son of his family, at the very beginning of a wave from the province with 34% of families in the region having a relative in New York

City by 1990.[15] He arrived to New York City at the earliest stages of this wave in 1968 when he was 17 years old, though he had falsified documents to show that he was 18 years old and, therefore, was able to travel as an adult on his own. Yet, he didn't arrive to the United States for a vacation or to go to school—he arrived to work, which is what he did. This meant that, unlike my mother, he never received formal education in English and learned it through work and through navigating life in an English-dominant society. Soon after arriving he met my mother at one of her cousin's parties, and they would eventually marry in 1972.

In short, my parents were both geopolitically positioned as residing in the Third World within the context of Cold War politics, as an extension of an early imperial relationship between the United States and Latin America. Both of their countries of origin had been discursively produced as backward and in need of modernization because of racial, linguistic, and cultural inferiorities. Efforts to promote this modernization, either directly or in conjunction with the United States, led to their eventual displacement, and they would eventually find one another in New York City. While sharing certain geopolitical positions in relation to the United States and the world, as children it is unlikely that they would have seen each other as members of the same community and would have likely identified most strongly with their nationalities. This changed upon their arrival to New York City, where they were now living in the same community and navigating the same spaces because of a shared language. While their shared use of Spanish was part of what brought them together, it was also part of what continued to racialize them in the United States, where they were now part of a "Spanish-dominant" community that was described through the culture of poverty discourse. In this way, while the culture of poverty discourse was a continuation of US colonialism and imperialism in Latin America, increasing numbers of displaced persons created new identifications in relation to one another because of their shared language and experiences of racialization, which served to counter these broader discourses through everyday acts, including raising families that sought to sustain cultural and linguistic traditions, as well as broader political mobilization for more equitable access through efforts such as demands for bilingual education.[16]

Yet, it is important to reiterate the fact that this geopolitical position was made possible through the erasure of Blackness and Indigeneity. More specifically, on the 1950 US Census undertaken the year that my mother was born, she and her parents had been officially classified as white by the census takers. In addition, the official racial designation that my father received on his passport was "mestizo." They brought these racial designations with them to the United States and as a result primarily experienced racialization through their Spanish-language use—a racialization process that I would also inherit. My family's experience connected with a broader universalization of a white and mestizo geopolitical position into what it meant to be Latinx in the United States. This would provide the ideological foundation for the discursive framing of the primary challenges of Latinxs in the United States as linguistic rather than racial, with bilingual education being well positioned to address these challenges. This framing continues to frame the field of bilingual education and Latinx studies in ways that fail to account for the fact that Black and Indigenous people from Latin America confront racial oppression that extends beyond the racialization of their language practices before their arrival to the United States, and they continue to experience this broader racialization upon their arrival.[17] As will be seen below, it was also the discourse that shaped how I made sense of my own racialization, as well as my professional trajectory into bilingual education.

My Raciolinguistic Socialization into Latinidad in the United States

My raciolinguistic socialization[18] was situated within the broader colonial histories that brought my parents to New York City and framed their Spanish-language use within broader discourses of the culture of poverty that framed it as, at best, a temporary tool for the development of English. This transitional mindset is reflected in the shifting language patterns of my family across time. Before having children, Spanish was the primary language that they used with one another, as well as within the broader community since most of their neighbors were bilingual. This continued when my oldest brother was born in 1973, though it quickly changed when my parents decided to move to a predominantly white working-class neighborhood in Philadelphia in 1977, which one could imagine was not an option available to Black and Indigenous people with origins in Latin America for a range of different reasons. After this move, my older brother quickly began to prefer English over Spanish and eventually stopped using Spanish completely after he began school.

By the time I was born in 1981 as the third of what would eventually become four children, English was the primary language used by my siblings and would, in turn, be the primary language I used. This did not mean that Spanish disappeared from our home. My parents continued to communicate with one another primarily through Spanish. In addition, they typically communicated with us bilingually, with my father typically using more Spanish than English, and my mother more English than Spanish. As a young child, I assumed that everybody communicated the way that my family did. It was only when I began to attend school that I realized that my family was different and that while I identified as an English speaker, some of the words that I assumed were English were labeled as Spanish by many of my peers and teachers. While I was soon able to reserve these words for home and produce "pure" English with friends and teachers, something about my English was still deemed strange. Many of my peers continued to insist that I had a "funny accent." My attempts at producing "pure" English were an apparent failure due to continued "contamination" from Spanish.

My apparent lack of Spanish-language abilities baffled people even more than my funny English. Students in my high school Spanish class often complained that because I was Latino I had an unfair advantage because I already spoke Spanish. When I told them that I did not speak Spanish very well, they looked at me quizzically and demanded to know how I could be "Spanish" and not speak the language. It was not just my classmates who thought this. One day a substitute teacher chastised me for not wanting to expand my horizons by learning an actual foreign language. He couldn't seem to understand that I might be taking Spanish as a way of reconnecting with my heritage, nor could he fathom that English might be my primary language. To him, I was clearly a Spanish speaker who wanted an easy A. The irony was that Spanish was not an easy A for me since the Spanish I had been exposed to at home was different from the idealized standardized Spanish of monolingual speakers from Spain and Latin America that was the focus of our textbook. I concluded that while my non-Latinx peers were exposed to proper Spanish, I had been exposed to "Spanglish" on a regular basis in my home and community, and that this placed me at a disadvantage in relation to them.

In short, my raciolinguistic socialization as a child consisted primarily of messages about the inadequacy of both my English and my Spanish. While I identified as a native English speaker, many of my interlocutors refused to accept that this could be possible—even after I had learned to reserve words that were part of my family language that most of my interlocutors perceived as Spanish solely for home and when engaging with other Latinxs. In addition, while my non-Latinx classmates may have thought that my being a Latino gave me an unfair advantage in Spanish class, the reality is that the Spanish knowledge that I did bring into the classroom was, at best, ignored by my teachers and, at worst, was framed as incorrect because of its failure to adhere to idealized monolingual norms. In this way, I was framed as lacking legitimacy in my use of either of the two languages I grew up with. While at the time, I attributed this positioning to my own personal inadequacies, a raciolinguistic genealogical perspective situates these experiences within broader ideologies of languagelessness that have been used to racialize US Latinxs since the beginning of the US colonial relationship with Mexican Americans in the American Southwest.[19]

Resisting My Professional Funneling into Bilingual Education

When I decided to pursue a college degree in educational studies, my initial desire was to use this degree as a way of improving the education of Latinx students. I had never heard of bilingual education, nor would I have considered it an area of much relevance to meeting the needs of Latinx students since all the Latinx friends and relatives I grew up with were proficient in English (or so I thought). Yet, I soon realized that it was one of the few research areas that centered the educational needs of Latinx students. At the time I assumed it was because bilingual education provided a solution to the problems confronting Latinx students and that for this reason it was under political attack by conservative political opponents. While this may be true to some extent, what I didn't realize at the time was that I was being professionally funneled into bilingual education because of funding mechanisms connected to the culture of poverty that had helped to fund the emergence of bilingual education as a cohesive body of research that pointed to the benefits of these programs. Of particular note here was the Title VII fellowship program that was used to support predominantly Latinx bilingual educators in pursuing doctoral degrees that they could then use to create and shape the growing number of bilingual teacher education programs that were also being supported by BEA funds.[20] This not only contributed to the emergence of bilingual education as a legitimate research agenda within schools of education, but also paved the way for increasing numbers of Latinx academics and allies who, while perhaps most interested in improving the education of Latinx students, were funneled into a focus on bilingual education because of the increased resources received to further pursue their education in this area.

While not necessarily individually on board with the verbal deprivation theory that shaped the ideological foundation of the BEA, the growing number of bilingual education researchers had to navigate their position in relation to it. As documented previously in this book, a dominant framing that would gain currency in the field that attempted to balance verbal deprivation theory with more culturally and affirming pedagogical strategies was that coercive relations of power had led to subtractive bilingualism for many Latinx students where Spanish was gradually replaced with English, and that additive bilingualism could help to challenge these coercive relations of power by ensuring that these students develop academic language in Spanish that they could then transfer to English.[21] In conjunction with this framing was the argument that dual-language programs that brought together Spanish-dominant and English-dominant students were most effective at ensuring that Latinx students developed a strong basis for academic language in Spanish that they would be able to transfer to English.[22]

Applying this framing to my own life, I began to wonder if many of my Latinx friends and relatives had, in fact, been truly English proficient, or if perhaps they had mastered social but not academic language, which might explain why many of them didn't do as well in school as I had. Ironically, I had gone from being a Latino child whose English and Spanish were deemed as not good enough to a Latino adult questioning the English and Spanish abilities of my Latinx friends, relatives, and students. I am now embarrassed about how easily I began to question the legitimacy of the language practices of friends and relatives with whom I had communicated in English my entire life. I am even more embarrassed by the ways that I sought to apply this framework to my students officially classified as "long-term English learners," as discussed previously in this book. In many ways, I became the Latinx professional seeking proximity to whiteness by positioning myself as a community leader seeking to fix the supposed cultural and linguistic deficiencies of Latinx students, which I have been critiquing in this book.

Yet, it was my own personal experiences with linguistic marginalization that gradually made me begin to question this narrative. I began to wonder how it was possible for students whom I observed using English and Spanish on a daily basis to be simultaneously English learners and deficient in Spanish. Why was the bilingualism of my students deemed not good enough? How did this connect to my own experiences as a US Latino who had always been made to feel that my bilingualism was not good enough? It was these questions that would eventually lead me to pursue doctoral studies in Urban Education at the CUNY Graduate Center in New York City.

Based on my interests in issues of language in education, I soon connected with Ofelia García, who would become my dissertation advisor. As a Cuban American who has dedicated her career to serving the Latinx community, she was a pioneer in educating students bilingually before bilingual education became institutionalized within the discourses of verbal deprivation theory. She was professionally funneled into the institutionalized form of bilingual education when she was appointed as a professor in City College's bilingual teacher education program, which would eventually lead her to the Graduate Center, in my second year of doctoral studies, as an internationally recognized scholar in bilingual education.[23] In the fall of 2008, I took my first course with her, in which she shared with us page proofs of what would become her groundbreaking book, *Bilingual Education in the 21st Century: A Global Perspective*, where she would lay out her original theorization of the translanguaging theory that she has continued to develop over the past fifteen years.[24] What Ofelia made clear to us in that course, which in subsequent years she has increasingly leaned into, is that translanguaging is not solely a linguistic or educational theory, but a political stance that centers the knowledge and meaning-making of racialized bilingual communities as a starting point for reimagining linguistic and educational theory and practice.[25]

It was this political stance that I brought to conversations that I began to have with my friend Jonathan Rosa, whom I had met as an undergraduate and had taken courses in Educational Studies with. At the time, it seemed as if our professional trajectories would be quite distinct, with Jonathan pursuing Educational Studies in conjunction with Linguistics and immediately entering a doctoral program in Linguistic Anthropology post-graduation and me pursuing Educational Studies in conjunction with Political Science and immediately becoming a classroom teacher post-graduation. Yet, what I have come to realize through this raciolinguistic genealogy is that our trajectories were never as distinct as they appeared. Like me, Jonathan had initially gravitated toward the study of language as one of the few viable disciplinary options for understanding his own experiences of racialization as a US Latinx. Also like me, his own personal experiences as a Latino had made him increasingly aware of the limitations of adopting a purely linguistic frame to understanding the racialization of Latinidad. This would eventually lead to our collaborations toward creating a raciolinguistic perspective that we would use to call into question contemporary approaches to language education.[26]

In our first collaboration in 2015, we called into question the notion of appropriateness that undergirds dominant approaches to language education. It is here that we first introduced the concept of raciolinguistic ideologies to describe how race and language co-construct with one another in ways that overdetermine racialized communities to be engaged in inappropriate language practices even when engaged in communicative practices that would be perceived as appropriate if used by white speakers. We have since developed this perspective into a conceptual framework that can be used to systematically study the co-construction of language and race.[27] At the core of these efforts has been a shift in focus away from what racialized speakers purportedly do with language to what the white listening subject perceives, and consequently the focus of intervention away from modifying the language practices of racialized communities to challenging these hegemonic modes of perception. Adopting the raciolinguistic genealogical stance in this book has helped me to further connect the institutionalization of bilingual education in the post–Civil Rights era with broader histories of white settler colonialism and anti-Blackness. I have also been able to connect this with a broader global geopolitical reconfiguration of race where certain racialized people would receive contingent proximity to whiteness in exchange for maintaining the colonial logics that have produced their racialization to begin with.

In short, while broader sociohistorical forces professionally funneled me into bilingual education, the marginalization that I experienced as a US Latino pushed me into eventually resisting this professional funneling by developing a conceptual and methodological approach that could be used to connect the dominant discourses within bilingual education research, policy, and practice with broader colonial histories that have shaped not only my own family history, but also the geopolitics of the world. While doing this has allowed me to call into question the basic assumptions of the dominant framing of bilingual education, it has also pointed to the possibility of thinking through the role that a politics of language might play in the creation of new forms of solidarity that seek to develop new, more inclusive ways of being in the world that are not premised on the dehumanization of any populations.[28]

As I have presented my thinking that has gotten me to this point over the years, I have encountered many senior Latinx scholars who shared stories about how they have made similar points throughout the years and have felt marginalized in the field because of their more radical position in relation to the hegemonic consensus around academic language and uncritical support for dual-language education. This can be seen in the fact that while my work has been critiqued by some prominent senior scholars in bilingual education,[29] it has been taken up by prominent Latinx scholars in their continued efforts at critiquing the hegemonic narrative of the field that they have been enacting throughout their careers.[30] This indicates that bilingual education scholarship has never been just one thing, and that there have always been scholars working to imagine decolonial approaches to bilingual education. I don't want this statement to be used to sugarcoat the reality that colonial logics remain hegemonic in the field and have historically and continue to be used to marginalize Latinx scholars, teachers, students, and communities. I also do not want these efforts to be romanticized, since working to imagine decolonial approaches within fundamentally colonial institutions will always be fraught and contradictory. Nor do I wish to imply that this work is only being done in academia, since I have strong personal connections with many bilingual education teachers, administrators, and policymakers working to enact decolonial approaches in their areas of control. Nevertheless, I think it is fitting, as a current Latino academic who studies bilingual education, to end this book recognizing the scholars who were able to use bilingual education as a point of entry for opening previously closed doors and not only ensuring to keep them open for those of us who followed, but encouraging us to continue to grapple with our ethical responsibility as Latinx scholars to navigate and resist the colonial logics that permeate the institutions we have been offered contingent acceptance into. I hope that the efforts that I have undertaken in this book are able to continue in that tradition by opening new pathways to imagine decolonial futures in bilingual education as part of the broader political project of developing new, more inclusive ways of being and knowing.

Notes

Chapter 1

1. Because these data were collected as part of an IRB-approved study, pseudonyms are used for both schools.
2. Eugene P. Ericksen, David Bartelt, Patrick Feeney, Gerald Foeman, Sherri Grasmuck, Maurren Martella, William Rickle, Robert Spencer, and David Webb, *The State of Puerto Rican Philadelphia* (Philadelphia: Institute for Public Policy Studies, 1985), p. 20.
3. Carmen Whalen, *From Puerto Rico to Philadelphia: Puerto Rican Workers and Postwar Economies* (Philadelphia: Temple University Press, 2001).
4. Stephen Sansweet, "Language Is a Big Barrier to Latin Newcomer," *Philadelphia Inquirer*, June 4, 1968, p. 15.
5. Sansweet, "Language Is a Big Barrier to Latin Newcomer," p. 15.
6. John Spencer, *In the Crossfire: Marcus Foster and the Troubled History of American School Reform* (Philadelphia: University of Pennsylvania Press, 2012).
7. The School-Community Coordinating Team, *School District of Philadelphia Great Cities School Improvement Program* (Philadelphia: School District of Philadelphia, 1965), p. 24.
8. School-Community Coordinating Team, *School District of Philadelphia Great Cities School Improvement Program*, p. 2.
9. School-Community Coordinating Team, *School District of Philadelphia Great Cities School Improvement Program*, p. 6.
10. Carl Bereiter and Siegfried Engelmann, *Teaching Disadvantaged Children in the Preschool* (Englewood Cliffs, NJ: Prentice-Hall, 1966).
11. School-Community Coordinating Team, *School District of Philadelphia Great Cities School Improvement Program*, p. 84.
12. School-Community Coordinating Team, *School District of Philadelphia Great Cities School Improvement Program*, p. 67.
13. William Jones, "Two Exchange Teachers Help to Break Language Barrier for Puerto Ricans," *Philadelphia Bulletin*, March 18, 1964.
14. "Schools Aid Puerto Ricans," *Philadelphia Inquirer*, June 6, 1965.
15. Carmen Sylvia Garcia, *Study of the Initial Involvement in the Social Services by the Puerto Rican Migrants in Philadelphia* (Doctoral dissertation, University of Pennsylvania, 1968).
16. Alfred Klimkcke, "Bilingual Plan Perks Up Pupils in City Schools," *Philadelphia Inquirer*, November 19, 1967, p. 24.

17. Kenzo Sung, "'Accentuate the Positive, Eliminate the Negative': Hegemonic Interest Convergence, Racialization of Latino Poverty, and the 1968 Bilingual Education Act," *Peabody Journal of Education, 92*, no. 3: 302–321
18. Rubén Donato, *The Other Struggle for Equal Schools: Mexican Americans during the Civil Rights Era* (Albany: State University of New York Press, 1997).
19. Sonia Song-Ha Lee, *Building a Latino Civil Rights Movement: Puerto Ricans, African Americans, and the Pursuit of Racial Justice in New York City* (Chapel Hill: University of North Carolina Press, 2014).
20. Sarah Bradlee Apt, *Community Movements, Politicization, and Bilingual Education in North Philadelphia* (Undergraduate thesis, Swarthmore College, 2010).
21. Sansweet, "Language Is a Big Barrier to Latin Newcomer," p. 15.
22. Sung, "'Accentuate the Positive, Eliminate the Negative.'"
23. Robert M. Offenberg, *Title VII Bilingual Project: Let's Be Amigos Evaluation of the First Year, 1969–1970* (Philadelphia: School District of Philadelphia, 1970), p. ii.
24. Francis Sutman, Eleanor Sandstrom, and Francis Shoemaker, *Educating Personnel for Bilingual Settings: Present and Future* (Philadelphia: American Association of Colleges for Teacher Education, 1979), p. 17.
25. Sutman, Sandstrom, and Shoemaker, *Educating Personnel for Bilingual Settings*, p. 16.
26. John Gillepsie, "City's New Spanish-Speaking School Faces Severe Overcrowding," *Philadelphia Bulletin*, September 11, 1969.
27. Dale Mezzacappa, "Learning in 2 languages: Advantage or Hindrance? *Philadelphia Inquirer*, October 6, 1987.
28. Ericksen et al., *The State of Puerto Rican Philadelphia.*
29. Robert Offenberg, Carlos Rodriguez-Acosta, and Bob Epstein, *Evaluation of the Potter-Thomas Bilingual-Bicultural Magnet Elementary School Project* (Philadelphia: Office of Research Planning and Evaluation, 1983), p. 5.
30. Offenberg, Rodriguez-Acosta, and Epstein, *Evaluation of the Potter-Thomas Bilingual-Bicultural Magnet Elementary School Project*, p. 4.
31. Melissa Cahnmann, "Thirty Years of Language-in-Education Policy and Planning: Potter Thomas Bilingual School in Philadelphia," *Bilingual Research Journal, 22*, no. 1 (1998), p. 68.
32. Interview with William Zinn, conducted January 25, 1988 (Nancy Hornberger Personal Archives).
33. Nancy Hornberger, "Extending Enrichment Bilingual Education: Revisiting Typologies and Redirecting Policy," in *Foccusschrift in Honor of Joshua A. Fishman on the Occasion of His 65th Birthday*, edited by Ofelia García (Philadelphia: John Benjamins, 1991), p. 228.
34. Interview with William Zinn, January 25, 1988.
35. Marisol Bello, "2-Language School Marks Its 25th Year: After a Long Uphill Struggle, It's Now a Model for Future," *Philadelphia Daily News*, November 21, 1994.
36. Hornberger, "Extending Enrichment Bilingual Education," p. 228.
37. Lauren Gilman, *Bilingual Education from Policy to Practice: An In-Depth Look at the Potter-Thomas School* (Undergraduate thesis, Bryn Mawr College, Bryn Mawr, 1988), p. 43.

38. Cheryl Micheau, *Ethnic Identity and Ethnic Maintenance in the Puerto Rican Community of* Philadelphia (Doctoral dissertation, University of Pennsylvania, Philadelphia), p. 520
39. Bello, "2-Language School Marks Its 25th Year."
40. Cahnmann, "Thirty Years of Language-in-Education Policy and Planning."
41. Robert Offenberg, "Evolution of a Bilingual Evaluation," *American Educational Research Association Annual Meeting* (New Orleans, 1973), p. 4.
42. Offenberg, "Evolution of a Bilingual Evaluation," pp. 3–4.
43. Interview with Felicita Melendez, conducted January 25, 1988 (Nancy Hornberger Personal Archives).
44. Interview with William Zinn, January 25, 1988.
45. Interview with William Zinn, January 25, 1988.
46. Steve Twomey, "How Schools Ranked in Achievement Tests," *Philadelphia Inquirer*, August 22, 1975.
47. David Kushma, "Critics Hit Schools' 2-Language Approach," *Philadelphia Bulletin*, June 11, 1978.
48. Mary Bishop, Thomas Ferrick, Jr., and Donald Kimelman, "What Is CAT? A Measure of Reading and Math Skills," *Philadelphia Inquirer*, September 5, 1981.
49. Bello, "2-Language School Marks Its 25th Year."
50. Dale Mezzacappa, "Union Opposition Alters Education Reform Plan in Philadelphia," *Philadelphia Inquirer*, April 6, 1995.
51. Brian Gill, Ron Zimmer, Jolley Christman, and Suzanne Blanc, *State Takeover, School Restructuring, Private Management, and Student Achievement in Philadelphia* (Santa Monica, CA: RAND, 2007), p. xi.
52. Gill, Zimmer, Christman, and Blanc, *State Takeover, School Restructuring*, p. 7.
53. Gill, Zimmer, Christman, and Blanc, *State Takeover, School Restructuring*, p. 11.
54. John Chubb, "The First Few Years of Edison Schools: Ten Lessons in Getting to Scale," *Expanding the Reach of Educational Reform: Perspectives from Leaders in the Scale-Up of Educational Interventions*, edited by Thomas K. Glennan, Susan J. Bodilly, Jolene R. Galegher, and Kerri A. Kerr (Santa Monica, CA: RAND, 2004), p. 512
55. Robert Slavin and Nancy Madden, *One Million Children: Success for All* (Thousand Oaks, CA: Corwin Press, 2001); Ester J. de Jong, "Effective Bilingual Education: From Theory to Academic Achievement in a Two-Way Bilingual Program," *Bilingual Research Journal, 26*, no. 1 (2002), p. 72.
56. Gill, Zimmer, Christman, and Blanc, *State Takeover, School Restructuring*, pp. 29–31.
57. Dale Mezzacappa, "Edison Schools Say Test System Surmounts Obstacles," *Philadelphia Inquirer*, December 18, 2002, B1.
58. Mensah Dean, "1 More Year, 1 More Chance—School-Manager Funding OK'd," *Philadelphia Daily News*, June 28, 2007.
59. Mensah Dean, "Private Managers Lose 6 Schools," *Philadelphia Daily News*, June 19, 2008.
60. "SIG LEA Application for Turnaround Model for Potter-Thomas," 2009, p. 14.
61. Luke Harold, "Potter-Thomas Students Excited by Their New Library," *Philadelphia Inquirer*, October 23, 2010. https://www.inquirer.com/philly/news/local/20101023_Potter-Thomas_students_excited_by_their_new_library.html.

62. James Crawford, *Bilingual Education: History, Politics, Theory and Practice* (Los Angeles: Bilingual Educational Services, 1999); Nancy Hornberger, "Nichols to NCLB: Local and Global Perspectives on US Language Education Policy," in *Imagining Multilingual Schools*, edited by Ofelia García, Tove Skutnabb-Kangas, and María Torres-Guzmán (Clevedon, UK: Multilingual Matters, 2006), 223–237; Sarah Moore, *A History of Bilingual Education in the US: Examining the Politics of Language Policymaking* (Bristol, UK: Multilingual Matters, 2021).
63. Cahnmann, "Thirty Years of Language-in-Education Policy and Planning."

Chapter 2

1. Michel Foucault, "Nietzsche, Genealogy, History," in *The Foucault Reader*, edited by Paul Rabinow (New York: Pantheon Books, 1984), p. 85.
2. Michel Foucault, *The History of Sexuality*, volume 1 (New York: Random House, 1978).
3. Sylvia Wynter, "Unsettling the Coloniality of Being/Power/Truth/Freedom: Towards the Human, after Man, Its Overrepresentation—An Argument," *The New Centennial Review, 3*, no. 3 (2003), p. 319.
4. Wynter, "Unsettling the Coloniality of Being/Power/Truth/Freedom," p. 266.
5. Patrick Wolfe, "Settler Colonialism and the Elimination of the Native," *Journal of Genocide Research, 8*, no. 4 (2006): 387–409.
6. Michel Foucault, *Society Must Be Defended: Lectures at the Collége de France 1975–1976* (New York: Picador, 2006), pp. 239–240.
7. Foucault, *Society Must Be Defended*, p. 241.
8. Wynter, "Unsettling the Coloniality of Being/Power/Truth/Freedom," p. 266.
9. Zakiyyah Iman Jackson, *Becoming Human: Matter and Meaning in an Antiblack World* (New York: New York University Press, 2020), p. 4.
10. Ann Stoler, *Race and the Education of Desire: Foucault's History of Sexuality and the Colonial Order of Things* (Durham, NC: Duke University Press, 1995).
11. Cedric J. Robinson, *Black Marxism: The Making of the Black Radical Tradition* (Chapel Hill: University of North California Press, 1983); Branwen Gruffydd Jones, "Race in the Ontology of International Order," *Political Studies, 56*, no. 4 (2008): 907–927; Jodi Melamed, "Racial Capitalism," *Critical Ethnic Studies, 1*, no. 1 (2015): 76–85.
12. Cheryl Harris, "Whiteness as Property," *Harvard Law Review, 106*, no. 8 (1993): 1710–1791.
13. Wynter, "Unsettling the Coloniality of Being/Power/Truth/Freedom."
14. Richard Delgado and Jean Stefanic, *Critical Race Theory: An Introduction* (New York: New York University Press, 2001).
15. Jodi Melamed, *Represent and Destroy: Rationalizing Violence in the New Racial Capitalism* (Minneapolis: University of Minnesota Press, 2011), p. 37.
16. Eduardo Bonilla-Silva, *Racism without Racists: Colorblind Racism and the Persistence of Racial Inequality in America* (Lanham, MD: Rowman & Littlefield, 2014).
17. Mari J. Matsuda, "Looking to the Bottom: Critical Legal Studies and Reparations," *Harvard Civil Rights-Civil Liberties Law Review, 22*, no. 2 (1987): 323–399; Harris,

"Whiteness as Property"; Charles Henry, *Long Overdue: The Politics of Racial Reparations* (New York: New York University Press, 2009).

18. Nelson Flores and Jonathan Rosa, "Undoing Appropriateness: Raciolinguistic Ideologies and Language Diversity in Education," *Harvard Educational Review, 85*, no. 2 (2015): 149–171.
19. Stephen Greenblatt, *Learning to Curse: Essays in Early Modern Culture* (Cambridge, MA: Harvard University Press, 1990); Gabriella Veronelli, "The Coloniality of Language: Race, Expressivity, Power and the Darker Side of Modernity," *Wagadu, 13* (2015): 108–34.
20. Frantz Fanon, *Black Skin, White Masks* (London: Pluto Press, 1967); Marcyliena Morgan, *Language, Discourse, and Power in African American Culture* (Cambridge: Cambridge University Press, 2002); Cécile B. Vigoroux, "The Discursive Pathway of Two Centuries of Raciolinguistic Stereotyping: 'Africans as Incapable of Speaking French," *Language in Society, 46*, no. 1 (2017): 5–21.
21. Walter Mignolo, *Local Histories/Global Designs: Coloniality, Subaltern Knowledges, and Border Thinking* (Princeton, NJ: Princeton University Press, 2000); Lisa Lowe, "The Intimacies of Four Continents," in *Haunted by Empire: Geographies of Intimacy in North American History*, edited by Ann Laura Stoler (Durham, NC: Duke University Press, 2006), 191–212.
22. Walter Mignolo, *The Darker Side of the Renaissance: Literacy, Territoriality and Colonization* (Ann Arbor: University of Michigan Press, 1995); Alastair Pennycook, "Mother Tongues, Governmentality, and Protectionism," *International Journal of the Sociology of Language, 154* (2002): 11–28
23. Jacques Derrida, *Of Grammatology* (Baltimore, MD: Johns Hopkins University Press, 1974); Ayo Bamgbose, "Education in Indigenous Languages: The West African Model of Language Education," *The Journal of Negro Education, 52*, no. 1 (1983): 57–64; Pennycook, "Mother Tongues, Governmentality, and Protectionism"; Deborah Cameron, "Language Endangerment and Verbal Hygiene: History, Morality and Politics," in *Discourses of Endangerment: Ideology and Interest in the Defence of Language*, edited by Alexandre Duchêne and Monica Heller (London: Continuum, 2007), 268–285.
24. Tim Marr, "'Ya No Podemos Regresar al Quechua': Modernity, Identity, and Language Choice among Migrants in Urban Peru," in *History and Language in the Andes*, edited by Paul Heggarty and Adrian Pearce (New York: Palgrave Macmillian), 215–238.
25. Cameron, "Language Endangerment and Verbal Hygiene."
26. David Wallace, *Education for Extinction: American Indians and the Boarding School Experience, 1875–1928* (Lawrence: University of Kansas Press, 1995); K. Tsianina Lomawaima and Teresa McCarty, "When Tribal Sovereignty Challenges Democracy: American Indian Education and the Democratic Ideal," *American Educational Research Journal, 39*, no. 2 (2002): 279–305; Andrew Woolford, *The Benevolent Experiment: Indigenous Boarding Schools, Genocide, and Redress in Canada and the United States* (Lincoln: University of Nebraska Press, 2015).
27. Walter M. Brasch, *Black English and the Mass Media* (Amherst: University of Massachusetts Press, 1981), p. 5.

28. Morgan, *Language, Discourse, and Power in African American Culture*, p. 10.
29. Wynter, "Unsettling the Coloniality of Being/Power/Truth/Freedom."
30. L. Gómez, *Manifest Destinies: The Making of the Mexican American Race* (New York: New York University Press, 2018), p. 91.
31. Rubén Donato, *The Other Struggle for Equal Schools: Mexican Americans during the Civil Rights Era* (Albany: State University of New York Press, 1997).
32. Richard Valencia, *Dismantling Contemporary Deficit Thinking: Educational Thought and Practice*, (New York, Routledge, 2010).
33. Joel Spring, *Deculturalization and the Struggle for Equality: A Brief History of the Education of Dominated Cultures in the United States* (New York: Routledge, 2016).
34. Heather Williams, *Self-Taught: African American Education in Slavery and Freedom* (Chapel Hill: University of North Carolina Press, 2009).
35. Carlos Blanton, *The Strange Career of Bilingual Education in Texas, 1836–1981* (College Station: Texas A & M University Press, 2004).
36. Michael Omi and Howard Winant, *Racial Formation in the United States from the 1960s to the 1990s* (New York: Routledge, 1994), p. 99.
37. Howard Winant, *The New Politics of Race: Globalism, Difference, Justice* (Minneapolis: University of Minnesota Press, 2004), p. 112.
38. Melamed, *Represent and Destroy*, p. 26.
39. Harris, "Whiteness as Property," p. 1714.
40. Ujju Aggarwal, "The Ideological Architecture of Whiteness as Property in Educational Policy," *Educational Policy, 30*, no. 1 (2016): 128–152.
41. Richard Valencia, "The Mexican American Struggle for Equal Educational Opportunity in *Mendez v. Westminster*: Helping to Pave the Way for *Brown v. Board of Education*," *Teachers College Record, 107*, no. 3 (2005): 389–423.
42. Frederick Aguirre, Kristi Bowman, Gonzalo Mendez, Sylvia Mendez, Sandra Robbie, and Philippa Strum, "*Mendez vs. Westminster*: A Living History," *Michigan State Law Review, 2014* (2014), p. 419.
43. Oscar Lewis, *Five Families: Mexican Case Studies in the Culture of Poverty* (New York: Basic Books, 1959); Michael Harrington, *The Other America: Poverty in the United States* (New York: Macmillan, 1962); Daniel Moynihan, *The Negro Family: The Case for National Action* (Washington, DC: US Department of Labor, 1965); Oscar Lewis, *La Vida: A Puerto Rican Family in the Culture of Poverty—San Juan and New York* (New York: Random House, 1966).

Chapter 3

1. Richie Perez, "HS Revolt!," in *The Young Lords: A Reader* edited by Darrel Enck-Wanzer (New York: New York University Press, 2010), p. 28.
2. Mario Fantini, "Community Participation," in *The Politics of Urban Education*, edited by Marilyn Gittell and Alan Hevesi (New York: Frederick A. Praeger, 1969), p. 335.
3. Jodi Melamed, *Represent and Destroy: Rationalizing Violence in the New Racial Capitalism* (Minneapolis: University of Minnesota Press, 2011).

4. Joanne Leedom, "Voucher Plan Proposed to Bring Competition into Schools," *Christian Science Monitor*, February 18, 1970, p. 6.
5. *The Hyde Park Cadre as a Social System* (Chicago: Ford Training and Placement Program, 1970); Elizabeth Todd-Breland, "Barbara Sizemore and the Politics of Black Educational Achievement and Community Control, 1963–1975," *The Journal of African American History, 100*, no. 4 (2015): 636–662.
6. Fred Foley, "The Failure of Reform: Community Control and the Philadelphia Public Schools," *Urban Education, 10*, no. 4 (1976): 389–414.
7. William Stantley Rice, *Community Control of Schools: A Change Strategy for Altering the Lifestyle and Improving Educational Opportunities for Inner City Residents of Anacostia, a Washington DC Community* (Doctoral dissertation, University of Massachusetts, Amherst, 1980).
8. Armando Navarro, *The Cristal Experiment: A Chicano Struggle for Community Control* (Madison: University of Wisconsin Press, 1998).
9. Anthony DeJesús and Madeline Pérez, "From Community Control to Consent Decree: Puerto Ricans Organizing for Education and Language Rights in the 1960s and 70s in New York City," *Centro Journal, 11*, no. 2 (2009): 7–31; Tatiana M. F. Cruz "'We Took 'Em On': The Latino Movement for Educational Justice in Boston, 1965–1980," *Journal of Urban History, 1*, no. 2 (2017): 235–255.
10. Daniel M. Rosenfelt, "Indian Schools and Community Control," *Stanford Law Review*, 25 (1973): 489–550; John W. Tippeconnic III, "Tribal Control of American Indian Education: Observations since the 1960s with Implications for the Future," in *Next Steps: Research and Practice to Advance Indian Education*, edited by Karen Gayton Swisher and John W. Tippeconnic III (Charleston, SC: Clearinghouse on Rural Education and Small Schools), 33–50.
11. Alan Altshuler, *Community Control: The Black Demand for Participation in Large American Cities* (New York: Pegasus, 1970); Barbara Carter, *Pickets, Parents and Power: The Story behind the New York City Teacher's Strike* (New York: Citation Press, 1971).
12. Alyosha Goldstein, *Poverty in Common: The Politics of Community Action during the American Century* (Durham, NC: Duke University Press, 2012).
13. Tom Davies, *Mainstreaming Black Power* (Berkeley: University of California Press, 2017), p. 26.
14. Goldstein, *Poverty in Common*.
15. John Spencer, *In the Crossfire: Marcus Foster and the Troubled History of American School Reform* (Philadelphia: University of Pennsylvania Press, 2014).
16. Karen Ferguson, *Top Down: The Ford Foundation, Black Power, and the Reinvention of Racial Liberalism* (Philadelphia: University of Pennsylvania Press, 2013).
17. Jessica Harris, "Revolutionary Black Nationalism: The Black Panther Party," *The Journal of African American History, 86*, no. 3 (2001): 409–421.
18. Jeffrey O. G. Ogbar, "Rainbow Radicalism: The Rise of the Radical Ethnic Nationalism," in *The Black Power Movement: Rethinking the Civil Rights-Black Power Era*, edited by Peniel E. Joseph (New York: Routledge, 2013), 193–228; Laura Pulido, "Race, Class, and Political Activism: Black, Chicana/o, and Japanese-American

Leftists in Southern California, 1968–1978," *Antipode, 34*, no. 4 (2002): 762–788; Haunani-Kay Trask, "The Birth of the Modern Hawaiian Movement: Kalama Valley, O'ahu," *The Hawaiian Journal of History, 21* (1987): 126–153; Kathryn E. Wilson, "'Same Struggle, Same Fight': Yellow Seeds and the Asian American Movement in Philadelphia's Chinatown," *The Pennsylvania Magazine of History and Biography, 140*, no. 3 (2016): 423–425.

19. David Rogers, *110 Livingston Street: Politics and Bureaucracy in the New York City Schools* (New York: Percheron Press, 1968); Annette T. Rubinstein, *Schools against Children: The Case for Community Control* (New York: Monthly Review Press, 1970).
20. Mario Fantini, *What's Best for the Children? Resolving the Power Struggle between Parents and Teachers* (Garden City, NY: Anchor Press/Doubleday, 1974); Luis Fuentes, *The Fight against Racism in Our Schools: Puerto Rican, Black and Chinese Community Control in New York City* (New York: Pathfinder Press, 1973); Charles Wilson, "Year One at I.S. 201," *Social Policy*, (May–June 1970): 10–17.
21. Russell Rickford, *We Are an African People: Independent Education, Black Power, and the Radical Imagination* (New York: Oxford University Press, 2016).
22. Stokely Carmichael and Charles V. Hamilton, *Black Power: The Politics of Liberation in America* (New York: Vintage Books, 1967), p. 156.
23. Carmichael and Hamilton, *Black Power*, p. 29.
24. Carmichael and Hamilton, *Black Power*, p. 31.
25. Carmichael and Hamilton, *Black Power*, p. 18.
26. Carmichael and Hamilton, *Black Power*, p. 183.
27. Carmichael and Hamilton, *Black Power*, p. 44.
28. Carmichael and Hamilton, *Black Power*, p. 43.
29. Carmichael and Hamilton, *Black Power*, p. 38.
30. Carmichael and Hamilton, *Black Power*, p. 167.
31. Carmichael and Hamilton, *Black Power*, p. 166.
32. Carmichael and Hamilton, *Black Power*, p. 167.
33. Carmichael and Hamilton, *Black Power*, p. 171.
34. Randolph Hohle, *Race and the Origins of American Neoliberalism* (New York: Routledge, 2015).
35. Marilyn Gittell, *Local Control in Education: Three Demonstration School Districts in New York City* (New York: Frederick A. Praeger, 1972).
36. Maurice R. Berube and Marilyn Gittell, "The Struggle for Community Control," in *Confrontation at Ocean Hill-Brownsville: The New York School Strikes of 1968* (New York: Frederick A. Praeger, 1969), p. 4
37. Marilyn Gittell, "The Balance of Power and the Community School," in *Community Control of the Schools*, edited by Henry M. Levin (Washington, DC: Brookings Institute, 1970), p. 117.
38. Marilyn Gittell, "The Community and Its Schools," in *Schools against Children: The Case for Community Control*, edited by Annette T. Rubinstein (New York: Monthly Review Press, 1970), p. 247.
39. Maurice R. Berube, "Educational Achievement and Community Control," *Community Issues, 1* no. 1 (1968), p. 10.
40. Berube, "Educational Achievement and Community Control," p. 10.

41. Berube, "Educational Achievement and Community Control," p. 10.
42. Berube, "Educational Achievement and Community Control," p. 4.
43. Berube, "Educational Achievement and Community Control," p. 9.
44. Gittell, "The Community and Its Schools," p. 248.
45. Berube and Gittell, "The Struggle for Community Control," p. 6.
46. Gittell, "The Community and Its Schools," p. 249.
47. Maurice R. Berube, "The Trouble with Vouchers," *Community, 3,* no. 2 (1970), p. 1.
48. Berube, "The Trouble with Vouchers," p. 1.
49. Berube, "The Trouble with Vouchers," p. 1.
50. Berube, "The Trouble with Vouchers," p. 1.
51. Berube, "The Trouble with Vouchers," p. 2.
52. Berube, "The Trouble with Vouchers," p. 2.
53. Berube, "The Trouble with Vouchers," p. 2.
54. Berube, "The Trouble with Vouchers," p. 4.
55. Maurice R. Berube, "Bi-lingual Program in Ocean Hill," *Community, 1* no. 2 (1969), p. 5.
56. Annette Rubinstein, "Visiting Ocean Hill-Brownsville in November 1968 and May 1969," in *Schools against Children: The Case for Community Control* (New York: Monthly Review Press, 1970), p. 243.
57. Armando Navarro, *The Cristal Experiment: A Chicano Struggle for Community Control* (Madison: University of Wisconsin Press, 1998).
58. John Collier, "Survival at Rough Rock: A Historical Overview of the Rough Rock Demonstration School." *Anthropology & Education Quarterly, 19,* no. 3 (1988): 253–269.
59. Maurice R. Berube, "The Bereiter-Engelmann Method in Ocean Hill-Brownsville," *Community, 1,* no. 1 (1969), pp. 4–5.
60. Carl Bereiter and Siegfried Engelmann, *Teaching Disadvantaged Children in the Preschool* (Englewood Cliffs, NJ: Prentice-Hall, 1966).
61. William Labov, "The Logic of Nonstandard English," in *Report of the Twentieth Annual Round Table Meeting on Linguistics and Language Studies*, edited by James E. Alatis (Washington, DC: Georgetown University Press, 1970), 1–44.
62. Joshua Fishman and John Lovas, "Bilingual Education in Sociolinguistic Perspective," *TESOL Quarterly, 4,* no. 3 (1970): 215–222.
63. Iris Morales Luciano, "On Revolutionary Nationalism," in *The Young Lords: A Reader*, edited by Darrel Enck-Wanzer (New York: New York University Press, 2010), p. 134.
64. Berube, "Bi-lingual Program in Ocean Hill," p. 5.

Chapter 4

1. Waldemar A. Nielsen, *The Big Foundations* (New York: Columbia University Press, 1972).
2. Christine Marie Sierra, *The Political Transformation of a Minority Organization: The Council of La Raza, 1965–1980* (Doctoral dissertation, Stanford University, 1983), p. 174

3. Sierra, *The Political Transformation of a Minority Organization*.
4. Sierra, *The Political Transformation of a Minority Organization*, p. 195.
5. Karen Ferguson, *Top Down: The Ford Foundation, Black Power, and the Reinvention of Racial Liberalism* (Philadelphia: University of Pennsylvania Press, 2013); Herbert Haines, *Black Radicals and the Civil Rights Mainstream* (Knoxville: University of Tennessee Press, 1988); Charles V. Willie, "Philanthropic and Foundation Support for Blacks: A Case Study from the 1960s," *The Journal of Negro Education, 50*, no. 3 (1981): 270–284.
6. Benjamin Marquez, "Mexican-American Political Organizations and Philanthropy: Bankrolling a Social Movement," *Social Science Review, 77*, no. 3 (2003): 329–346; Sierra, *The Political Transformation of a Minority Organization*.
7. Victoria-María MacDonald and Benjamin Polk Hoffman, "'Compromising *la causa?*': The Ford Foundation and Chicano Intellectual Nationalism in the Creation of Chicano History, 1963–1977," *History of Education Quarterly, 52*, no. 2 (2012): 251–281.
8. Melvin Fox, *Language and Development: A Retrospective Survey of Ford Foundation Language Projects, 1952–1974*, Volume 1 (New York: Ford Foundation, 1975); J. L. Logan, "Coral Way: A Bilingual School," *TESOL Quarterly, 1*, no. 2 (1967): 50–54; Atilano Valencia, *Identification and Assessment of Ongoing Educational and Community Programs for Spanish Speaking People: A Report Submitted to the Southwest Council of La Raza* (Phoenix: Southwestern Cooperative Educational Lab, 1969); Ford Foundation Records Grants L-N, National Council of la Raza, Grant 06800564, Reel-2238–2239, Rockefeller Archive Center.
9. Diana Lemberg, "'The Universal Language of the Future': Decolonization, Development, and the American Embrace of Global English, 1945–1965," *Modern Intellectual History, 15*, no. 2 (2018): 561–592.
10. Robert Phillipson, "English Language Spread,". *International Journal of the Sociology of Language, 107* (1994): 7–24.
11. Fox, *Language and Development*.
12. Peter D. Bell, "The Ford Foundation as a Transnational Actor," *International Organization, 25*, no. 3 (1971): 465–478; Kathleen D. McCarthy, "From Cold War to Cultural Development: The International Cultural Activities of the Ford Foundation, 1950–1980," *Daedalus, 116*, no. 1 (1987): 93–117.
13. Ferguson, *Top Down: The Ford Foundation, Black Power, and the Reinvention of Racial Liberalism*; Dennis Lopez, "Cultivating Aztlán: Chicano (Counter)Cultural Politics and the Postwar American University," *American Studies, 58*, no. 1 (2019): 73–111.
14. Alejandro Portes and Cynthia Truelove, "Making Sense of Diversity: Recent Research on Hispanic Minorities in the United States," *Annual Review of Sociology, 13* (1987): 359–385; Sylvia Pedraza-Bailey, *Political and Economic Migrants in America: Cubans and Mexicans* (Austin: University of Texas Press, 1985).
15. James Crawford, *Hold Your Tongue: Bilingualism and the Politics of English Only* (Boston: Addison-Wesley, 1992); Josué M. González, "Coming of Age in Bilingual/Bicultural Education: A Historical Perspective," *Inequality in Education, 19* (1975): 5–17; Carlos J. Ovando, "Bilingual Education in the United States: Historical Development and Current Issues," *Bilingual Research Journal, 27* (2003): 1–24.

16. Logan, "Coral Way: A Bilingual School."
17. Mitchell Svirdidoff to McGeorge Bundy, May 14, 1968, Ford Foundation Records Grants L-N, National Council of La Raza, Grant 06800564, Reel 2238–2239, Rockefeller Archive Center.
18. Miguel F. Barragan, Henry Santiestevan, Bernardo Valdes, and Alex Mercure, *Proposal for the Southwest Council of La Raza*, Ford Foundation Records Grants L-N, National Council of la Raza, Grant 06800564, Reel-2238–2239, Rockefeller Archive Center, pp. 6–7.
19. Sierra, *The Political Transformation of a Minority Organization*; Emily Gantz McKay, *The National Council of La Raza: The First 25 Years* (Washington, DC: National Council of La Raza, 1993).
20. José Angel Gutiérrez, *The Making of a Chicano Militant* (Madison: University of Wisconsin Press, 1998); Armando Navarro, *Mexican American Youth Organization: Avant-Garde of the Chicano Movement in Texas* (Austin: University of Texas Press, 1995).
21. Joseph P. Kesler to the Ford Foundation, January 9, 1970, Ford Foundation Records Grants L-N, National Council of La Raza, Grant 06800564, Reel 2238–2239, Rockefeller Archive Center.
22. Navarro, *Mexican American Youth Organization.*
23. Ignacio M. García, "Mexican American Youth Organization: Precursors of Change in Texas," *Mexican American Studies & Research Center's Working Paper Series*, no. 8 (1987): 1–22.
24. Navarro, *Mexican American Youth Organization.*
25. Siobhan Oppenheimer to Samuel F. Tower, May 23, 1969, Ford Foundation Records Grants L-N, National Council of La Raza, Grant 06800564, Reel 2238–2239, Rockefeller Archive Center.
26. Navarro, *Mexican American Youth Organization.*
27. Navarro, *Mexican American Youth Organization.*
28. Henry B. Gonzalez to Siobhan Oppenheimer, November 21, 1968, Ford Foundation Records Grants L-N, National Council of La Raza, Grant 06800564, Reel 2238–2239, Rockefeller Archive Center.
29. R. N. Conolly to Henry Ford II, April 14, 1969, Ford Foundation Records Grants L-N, National Council of La Raza, Grant 06800564, Reel 2238–2239, Rockefeller Archive Center.
30. John L. Seiler to Ford Motor Company, May 19, 1969, Ford Foundation Records Grants L-N, National Council of La Raza, Grant 06800564, Reel 2238–2239, Rockefeller Archive Center.
31. Robert Gleichenhaus to Henry Ford II, April 12, 1969, Ford Foundation Records Grants L-N, National Council of La Raza, Grant 06800564, Reel 2238–2239, Rockefeller Archive Center.
32. García, "Mexican American Youth Organization: Precursors of Change in Texas," p. 13.
33. John L. Seiler to Ford Motor Company, May 19, 1969, Ford Foundation Records Grants L-N, National Council of La Raza, Grant 06800564, Reel 2238–2239, Rockefeller Archive Center.

34. García, "Mexican American Youth Organization: Precursors of Change in Texas."
35. The Ford Community Affairs Committee to McGeorge Bundy, May 6, 1969, Ford Foundation Records Grants L-N, National Council of La Raza, Grant 06800564, Reel 2238–2239, Rockefeller Archive Center.
36. Siobhan Oppenheimer to Samuel F. Tower, May 23, 1969, Ford Foundation Records Grants L-N, National Council of La Raza, Grant 06800564, Reel 2238–2239, Rockefeller Archive Center.
37. Siobhan Oppenheimer to Joseph L. Carvajal, November 19, 1969, Ford Foundation Records Grants L-N, National Council of La Raza, Grant 06800564, Reel 2238–2239, Rockefeller Archive Center.
38. McKay, *The National Council of La Raza;* Sierra, *The Political Transformation of a Minority Organization.*
39. Juan Gómez-Quiñones, *Chicano Politics, Reality and Promise,* 1940–1990 (Albuquerque: University of New Mexico Press, 1990).
40. Josué M. González, *Special Report: Short Answers to Common Questions about Bilingual Education* (Washington, DC: National Council of La Raza, 1981); Lori S. Orum and Raul Yzaguirre, "Secretary Bennett's Bilingual Education Initiative: Historical Perspectives and Implications," *La Raza Law Journal, 1* (1986): 225–249; Janet Schroyet-Portillo, *Civil Rights in Crisis: The Reagan Administration's Reforms* (Washington, DC: National Council of La Raza, 1984); Dorothy Waggoner, *Language Minority Children at Risk in America: Concepts, Definitions and Estimates* (National Council of La Raza, 1984): 1–19.
41. Rees Lloyd and Peter Montague, "Ford and La Raza: 'They Stole Our Land and Gave Us Powered Milk,'" *Ramparts Magazine* (September 1970): 10–18.
42. Mario T. García, *Memories of Chicano History: The Life and Narrative of Bert Corona* (Berkeley: University of California Press, 1994), p. 229.
43. Gutiérrez, *The Making of a Chicano Militant*, p. 118.
44. Arnoldo Garcia, "Toward a Left without Borders: The Story of the Center for Autonomous Social Action-General Brotherhood of Workers," *Monthly Review,* 54, no. 3 (2002): 69–78; García, *Memories of Chicano History*; Jorge Mariscal, "Left Turns in the Chicano Movement, 1965–1975," *Monthly Review, 54*, no. 3 (2002): 59–68; Carlos Muñoz, Jr., *The Chicano Movement: Mexican American History and the Struggle for Equality* (New York: Rosa Luxemburg Stiftung, 2013).
45. Gómez-Quiñones, *Chicano Politics, Reality and Promise.*
46. Ignacio M. García, *United We Win: The Rise and Fall of La Raza Unida Party* (Tucson: University of Arizona Press, 1989).
47. Armando Trujillo, *Chicano Empowerment and Bilingual Education: Movimiento Politics in Crystal City, Texas* (New York: Routledge, 1998).
48. Armando Navarro, *The Cristal Experiment: A Chicano Struggle for Community Control* (Madison: University of Wisconsin Press, 1998).
49. Trujillo, *Chicano Empowerment and Bilingual Education.*
50. García, *United We Win*; Muñoz, Jr., *The Chicano Movement.*
51. Annette Rubinstein, "Visiting Ocean Hill-Brownsville in November 1968 and May 1969," in *Schools against Children: The Case for Community Control* edited by Annette Rubinstein (New York: Monthly Review Press, 1970), 228–247.

52. Mario Fantini to Mitchell Sviridoff, February 1, 1968, Ford Foundation Records Grants Them-Tw, Two Bridges Neighborhood Council, Inc., Grant 06700427, Reel 2368, Rockefeller Archive Center.
53. Jill Rice, *The Aspira Story, 1961–1991* (New York: Aspira Association, 1991).
54. Louis Nuñez, "Reflections on Puerto Rican History: Aspira in the Sixties and the Coming of Age of the Stateside Puerto Rican Community," *Centro Journal, 21*, no. 2 (2009): 33–47.
55. Aspira of America, Incorporated Precis, 1971, Ford Foundation Records Grants A-B, Aspira Association, Inc., Grant 07200071, Reel R1748, Rockefeller Archive Center.
56. Nuñez, "Reflections on Puerto Rican History.
57. Ariel Arnau, "The Evolution of Leadership within the Puerto Rican Community of Philadelphia, 1950s–1970s, *The Pennsylvania Magazine, 136*, no. 1 (2012): 53–81; Carmen Whalen, "Bridging Homeland and Barrio Politics: The Young Lords in Philadelphia," in *The Puerto Rican Movement: Voices from the Diaspora*, edited by Andrés Torres and José E. Velázquez (Philadelphia: Temple University Press, 1998), 107–123.
58. Nelson Flores, "A Tale of Two Visions: Hegemonic Whiteness and Bilingual Education," *Educational Policy, 30*, no. 1 (2016): 13–38.
59. Whalen, "Bridging Homeland and Barrio Politics," p. 114.
60. A Concerned and Frustrated Parent to Big Frank, n.d., Box 20, Folder 5, Lighthouse Records 1893–2000, Historical Society of Pennsylvania; "Information and Education Projects," *A Single Spark* (Summer 1973), Flatfile, Lighthouse Records 1893–2000, Historical Society of Pennsylvania.
61. Arnau, "The Evolution of Leadership within the Puerto Rican Community of Philadelphia, 1950s–1970s."
62. Minutes of the Meeting of the Long Range Planning Committee, October 28, 1970, Lighthouse Records 1893–2000, Box 19, Folder 17, Historical Society of Pennsylvania.
63. Lou Antosh, "UF Halts Funding of Lighthouse Agency," *Philadelphia Daily News*, November 14, 1970.
64. Bobbi Granger-Jaffe, *War Breaks Out Around the Lighthouse Settlement: Toward a Theoretical Knowledge Base for Professional Social Work Practice*, 1980, December, Box 21, Folder 5, Lighthouse Records 1893–2000, Historical Society of Pennsylvania.
65. A Concerned and Frustrated Parent to Big Frank, n.d., Box 20, Folder 5, Lighthouse Records 1893–2000, Historical Society of Pennsylvania.
66. "Learn from Negative Example: Lessons from the Degeneration of the Puerto Rican Revolutionary Workers Organization," *Getting Together Supplement* (February 1977), https://www.marxists.org/history/erol/ncm-1/iwk-prrwo.pdf.
67. *Resolutions & Speeches, 1st Congress: Puerto Rican Revolutionary Workers Organization (Young Lords Party)* (1972).
68. Arnau, "The Evolution of Leadership within the Puerto Rican Community of Philadelphia, 1950s–1970s."
69. Richard J. Hiller to Luis Alvarez, October 4, 1974, Box 19, Folder 6, The Latino Project 1962–1985, Historical Society of Pennsylvania.

70. Memo: Conversation with Sister Francis Georgia, 29, July, 1976, Box 17, Folder 7, The Latino Project, 1962–1985, Historical Society of Pennsylvania.
71. Michael Kimmel, "¡You've Come a Long Way Bebé!" *Philadelphia Magazine* (August 1971), p. 97.
72. Robert Lear to Ms. Taracido, May 2, 1977, Puerto Rican Legal Defense and Education Fund 1973–1993, Box 52, Folder 12. Center for Puerto Rican Studies.
73. Jack Smyth, "Coalition Protests City Schools Cut of Bilingual Program," *Philadelphia Bulletin* (July 10, 1981).
74. Cheryl Micheau, *Ethnic Identity and Ethnic Maintenance in the Puerto Rican Community of Philadelphia* (Doctoral dissertation, University of Pennsylvania, 1990).

Chapter 5

1. Ralph Yarborough (TX), "Two Proposals for a Better Way of Life for Mexican-Americans of the Southwest," *Congressional Record* 113 (1967), p. 599.
2. Yarborough, "Two Proposals for a Better Way of Life," p. 599.
3. Yarborough, "Two Proposals for a Better Way of Life," pp. 599–600.
4. Carl Bereiter and Siegfried Engelmann, *Teaching Disadvantaged Children in the Preschool* (Englewood Cliffs, NJ: Prentice-Hall, 1966).
5. Gilbert Sanchez, *An Analysis of the Bilingual Education Act, 1967–68* (Doctoral dissertation, University of Massachusetts Amherst, 1973).
6. National Education Association, *The Invisible Minority: Report of the NEA-Tucson Survey on the Teaching of Spanish to the Spanish Speaking* (Washington, DC: National Education Association, 1966).
7. National Education Association, *The Invisible Minority*, p. 11.
8. Severo Gomez, "The Meaning and Implications of Bilingualism for Texas Schools," in *Improving Educational Opportunities of the Mexican-American: Proceedings of the First Texas Conference for the Mexican-American*, edited by Dwain M. Estes and David W. Darlings (Austin: Texas Education Agency, 1967), p. 46.
9. Aspira of New York, *"Hemos Trabajado Bien": A Report on the First National Conference on Puerto Ricans, Mexican Americans and Educators on the Special Educational Needs of Urban Puerto Rican Youth* (Washington, DC: US Department of Health, Education & Welfare, Office of Education, 1968), p. 18.
10. Aspira of New York, *"Hemos Trabajado Bien,"* p. 24.
11. Aspira of New York, *"Hemos Trabajado Bien,"* p. 58.
12. National Education Association, *The Invisible Minority*, p. 10.
13. National Education Association, *The Invisible Minority*, p. 13.
14. Planning Conference on Early Childhood Bilingual Education, April 19, 1967, Ford Foundation Records Grants U-Z, Yeshiva University, Grant 06700217, Reel 1878, Rockefeller Archive Center, p. 2.
15. Herschel T. Manuel, "The Spanish-Speaking Child in Texas Schools," in *Improving Educational Opportunities of the Mexican-American: Proceedings of the First Texas*

Conference for the Mexican-American, edited by Dwain M. Estes and David W. Darlings (Austin: Texas Education Agency, 1967), p. 78.

16. Manuel, "The Spanish-Speaking Child in Texas Schools," p. 79.
17. Atilano Valencia, *Identification and Assessment of Ongoing Educational and Community Programs for Spanish Speaking People: A Report Submitted to the Southwest Council of La Raza* (Phoenix: Southwestern Cooperative Educational Lab, 1969); Ford Foundation Records Grants L-N, National Council of la Raza, Grant 06800564, Reel-2238–2239, Rockefeller Archive Center, pp. 1–2.
18. Valencia, *Identification and Assessment of Ongoing Educational and Community Programs*; Ford Foundation Records Grants L-N, National Council of la Raza, Grant 06800564, Reel-2238–2239, Rockefeller Archive Center, p. 4.
19. Elliot Lewis Judd, *Factors Affecting the Passage of the Bilingual Education Act of 1967* (Doctoral dissertation, New York University, 1977).
20. Bilingual Education: Hearings before the Subcommittee on Bilingual Education of the Committee on Labor and Public Welfare, Senate, 90th Congress, Washington. DC, 1967, p. 37.
21. Sanchez, *An Analysis of the Bilingual Education Act, 1967–68*.
22. Bilingual Education: Hearings, p. 1.
23. Bilingual Education: Hearings, pp. 131–132.
24. Bilingual Education: Hearings, p. 44.
25. Bilingual Education: Hearings, p. 58.
26. Bilingual Education: Hearings, p 42.
27. Bilingual Education: Hearings, p. 40.
28. Bilingual Education: Hearings, p. 33.
29. Bilingual Education: Hearings, p. 41.
30. Bilingual Education: Hearings, p. 89.
31. Wayne Au, "Asian American Racialization, Racial Capitalism, and the Threat of the Model Minority," *Review of Education, Pedagogy, and Cultural Studies, 44*, no. 3 (2022), pp. 199–200.
32. Grace Guthrie, *A School Divided: An Ethnography of Bilingual Education in a Chinese Community* (Hillsdale, NJ: Lawrence Erlbaum, 1985); Lawrence Wright, "The Bilingual Education Movement at the Crossroads," *Phi Delta Kappan, 55*, no. 3 (1973): 183–186; Sung-Ock Sohn and Craig Merill, "The Korean/English Dual Language Program in the Los Angeles Unified School District," in *Heritage Language Education: A New Field Emerging*, edited by Donna Brinton, Olga Kagan, and Susan Bauckus (New York: Routledge, 2017), 269–288.
33. Stacey Lee, Nga-Wing Anjela Wong, and Alvin Alvarez, "The Model Minority and the Perpetual Foreigner: Stereotypes of Asian Americans," in *Asian American Psychology: Current Perspectives*, edited by Nita Tewari and Alvin Alvarez (New York: Lawrence Erlbaum, 2008), 69–84.
34. Kenzo K. Sung and Ayana Allen-Hardy, "Contradictory Origins and Racializing Legacy of the 1968 Bilingual Education Act: Urban Schooling, Anti-Blackness, and Oakland's 1996 Black English Language Education Policy," *University of Maryland Law Journal of Race, Religion, Gender and Class, 19*, no. 1 (2019): 44–80.

Chapter 6

1. Aspira Consent Decree Panels–City University Graduate Center, May 20, 1976, Ford Foundation Videotapes, 1962–1995, Box 1 Reel AV 10007, Rockefeller Archive Center, 37:58–38:47.
2. Aspira Consent Decree Panels–City University Graduate Center, May 20, 1976, Ford Foundation Videotapes, 1962–1995, Box 1 Reel AV 10007, Rockefeller Archive Center, 38:55–39:22.
3. Aspira Consent Decree Panels–City University Graduate Center, May 20, 1976, Ford Foundation Videotapes, 1962–1995, Box 1 Reel AV 10007, Rockefeller Archive Center, 39:45–40:37.
4. Kate Menken, Tatyana Kleyn, Laura Ascenzi-Moreno, Nabin Chae, Nelson Flores, and Alex Funk, *Meeting the Needs of Long Term English Language Learners in High School, Phase II* (New York: New York City Department of Education, 2009).
5. For a self-critique of the original framing of the study that provides some of the theoretical foundation for this book, see Nelson Flores, Tatyana Kleyn, and Kate Menken, "Looking Holistically in a Climate of Partiality: Identities of Students Labeled Long-Term English Language Learners," *Journal of Language, Identity & Education, 14*, no. 2 (2015): 113–132.
6. Office of Education, *Programs under Bilingual Education Act (Title VII, ESEA): Manual for Project Applicants and Grantees* (Washington, DC: Office of Education, 1971), p. 15.
7. Office of Education, *Programs under Bilingual Education Act (Title VII, ESEA)*, p. 16. Office of Education, *Programs under Bilingual Education Act (Title VII, ESEA)*, p. 15.
8. Office of Education, *Programs under Bilingual Education Act (Title VII, ESEA)*, p. 11.
9. Office of Education, *Programs under Bilingual Education Act (Title VII, ESEA)*, p. 44.
10. Office of Education, *Programs under Bilingual Education Act (Title VII, ESEA)*, p. 50.
11. Office of Education, *Programs under Bilingual Education Act (Title VII, ESEA)*, p. 56.
12. Herbert Teitelbaum and Richard J. Hiller, "Bilingual Education: The Legal Mandate," *Harvard Educational Review, 47*, no. 2 (1977): 138–170.
13. Office for Civil Rights, *Task Force Findings Specifying Remedies Available for Eliminating Past Educational Practices Ruled Unlawful under Lau v. Nichols* (Washington, DC: Office for Civil Rights, 1975).
14. Heidi Dulay and Marina Burt, "The Relative Proficiency of Limited English Proficient Students," *NABE Journal, 4*, no. 3 (1980), p. 14.
15. Office for Civil Rights, *Task Force Findings Specifying Remedies*.
16. Jeanne Sinclair, "'Starving and Suffocating': Evaluation Policies and Practices during the First 10 Years of the U.S. Bilingual Education Act," *International Journal of Bilingual Education and Bilingualism, 21*, no. 6 (2018): 710–728.
17. Heidi Dulay and Marina Burt, "Current State Level Trends in the Assessment of Language Minority Students: An Introduction," in *Georgetown University Round Table on Languages and Linguistics: Current Issues in Bilingual Education*, edited by James E. Alatis (Washington, DC: Georgetown University Press, 1980), p. 224.

18. Dulay and Burt, "The Relative Proficiency of Limited English Proficient Students," p. 6.
19. Dulay and Burt, "The Relative Proficiency of Limited English Proficient Students," pp. 16–17.
20. Dulay and Burt, "The Relative Proficiency of Limited English Proficient Students," p. 19.
21. Jim Cummins, "The Entry and Exit Fallacy in Bilingual Education," *NABE Journal, 4*, no. 3 (1980), p. 47.
22. Jim Cummins, "The Influence of Bilingualism on Cognitive Growth: A Synthesis of Research Findings and Explanatory Hypotheses," *Working Papers on Bilingualism*, no. 9 (1976), p. 22.
23. Cummins, "The Entry and Exit Fallacy in Bilingual Education," p. 28.
24. Jim Cummins, "Linguistic Interdependence and the Educational Development of Bilingual Children," *Review of Educational Research, 49*, no. 2 (1979), p. 236.
25. Cummins, "The Entry and Exit Fallacy in Bilingual Education," p. 39.
26. Cummins, "The Entry and Exit Fallacy in Bilingual Education," p. 48.
27. Cummins, "The Entry and Exit Fallacy in Bilingual Education," p. 48.
28. Cummins, "The Entry and Exit Fallacy in Bilingual Education," p. 26.
29. Harvey Rosenbaum, "The Development and Structure of the Language Skills Framework of the Student Placement System for Bilingual Programs," in *Georgetown University Round Table on Languages and Linguistics: Current Issues in Bilingual Education*, edited by James E. Alatis (Washington, DC: Georgetown University Press, 1980), p. 32.
30. Rosenbaum, "The Development and Structure of the Language Skills Framework," p. 41.
31. Rosenbaum, "The Development and Structure of the Language Skills Framework," p. 42.
32. Rosenbaum, "The Development and Structure of the Language Skills Framework," p. 43.
33. Michael Kirst, "Recent State Education Reform in the United States: Looking Backward and Forward," *Educational Administration Quarterly, 24*, no. 3 (1988): 319–328.
34. F. Howard Nelson, "The Assessment of English Language Proficiency: Standards for Determining Participation in Transitional Language Programs," *Journal of Law and Education, 15*, no. 1 (1986): 83–103.
35. Nancy Hornberger, "Nichols to NCLB: Local and Global Perspectives on US Language Education Policy," in *Imagining Multilingual Schools: Languages in Education and Globalization*, edited by Ofelia García, Tove Skutnabb-Kangas, and Maria Torres-Guzmán (Clevedon, UK: Multilingual Matters, 2006), 223–237.
36. Richard Verdugo and Brittney Flores, "English-Language Learners: Key Issues," *Education and Urban Society, 39*, no. 2 (2007): 167–193.
37. Jamal Abedi, "The No Child Left Behind Act and English Language Learners: Assessment and Accountability Issues," *Educational Researcher, 33*, no. 1: 4–14.
38. Craig Deville and Micheline Chalhoub-Deville, "Accountability-Assessment under No Child Left Behind: Agenda, Practice and Future," *Language Testing, 28*, no. 3 (2011): 307–321.

39. Alison Bailey and Becky Huang, "Do Current Language Development/Proficiency Standards Reflect the English Needed for Success in School," *Language Testing, 28*, no. 3 (2011): 342–365.
40. Concepción Valdez, Jeff MacSwan, and Corrine Martínez, "Toward a New View of Low-Achieving Bilinguals: A Study of Linguistic Competence in Designated 'Semilinguals,'" *Bilingual Review/La Revista Bilingüe, 25*, no. 3 (2000): 238–248.
41. Laurie Olsen, *Reparable Harm: Fulfilling the Unkept Promise of Educational Opportunity for California's Long Term English Learners* (Long Beach: Californians Today, 2010), p. 26.
42. Olsen, *Reparable Harm*, p. 23.
43. Olsen, *Reparable Harm*, p. 23.
44. Olsen, *Reparable Harm*, p. 33.
45. Olsen, *Reparable Harm*, p. 35.
46. Jonathan Rosa, "Standardization, Racialization, Languagelessness: Raciolinguistic Ideologies across Communicative Contexts," *Journal of Linguistics Anthropology, 26*, no. 2 (2016): 162–183.
47. Olsen, *Reparable Harm*, p. 22.
48. Academic English Mastery Program, "How to Use the SEL Linguistic Screener."
49. Flores, Kleyn, and Menken, "Looking Holistically in a Climate of Partiality."
50. Nelson Flores and Sofia Chaparro, "What Counts as Language Education Policy? Developing a Materialist Anti-Racist Approach to Language Activism," *Language Policy, 17*, no. 3 (2018): 365–384.

Chapter 7

1. Rhody McCoy, *Analysis of Critical Issues and Incidents in the New York City School Crisis, 1967–1970, and Their Implications for Urban Education in the 1970's* (Doctoral dissertation, University of Massachusetts, Amherst, 1971), p. 149.
2. McCoy, *Analysis of Critical Issues and Incidents in the New York City School Crisis*, pp. 150–151.
3. McCoy, *Analysis of Critical Issues and Incidents in the New York City School Crisis*, p. 145.
4. McCoy, *Analysis of Critical Issues and Incidents in the New York City School Crisis*, p. 163.
5. McCoy, *Analysis of Critical Issues and Incidents in the New York City School Crisis*, p. 138.
6. Luis Fuentes, *Puerto Rican, Black and Chinese Community Control in New York City: The Fight against Racism in Our Schools* (New York: Pathfinder Press. 1973), p. 6.
7. Fuentes, *Puerto Rican, Black and Chinese Community Control in New York City*, p. 15.
8. Albert Shanker, "The Real Meaning of the New York City Teachers' Strike," *Phi Delta Kappan, 50*, no. 8 (1969), p. 436.
9. Shanker, "The Real Meaning of the New York City Teachers' Strike," p. 437.

10. Shanker, "The Real Meaning of the New York City Teachers' Strike," p. 439.
11. Fred Ferretti, "New York's Black Anti-Semitism Scare," *Columbia Journalism Review, 8, Fall* (1969), p. 19.
12. *Eyes on the Prize: Power! (1966–1968), PBS Videos: Chicago,* 48:25–48:41.
13. Sally Peterson, "Breaking the Bilingual Lobby's Stranglehold," in *The Failure of Bilingual Education*, edited by Jorge Amselle (Washington, DC: Center for Educational Opportunity, 1996), p. 78.
14. Peterson, "Breaking the Bilingual Lobby's Stranglehold," p. 79.
15. Linda Chavez, "Introduction: One Nation, One Language," in *The Failure of Bilingual Education*, edited by Jorge Amselle (Washington, DC: Center for Educational Opportunity, 1996), p. 7.
16. Rosa Castro Feinberg, "Bilingual Education in the United States: A Summary of Lau Compliance Requirements," *Language, Culture and Curriculum, 3*, no. 2 (1990): 141–152.
17. Herbert Teitelbaum and Richard J. Hiller, "Bilingual Education: The Legal Mandate," *Harvard Educational Review, 47*, no. 2 (1977): 138–169.
18. Teitelbaum and Hiller, "Bilingual Education: The Legal Mandate," p. 146.
19. Rachel Moran, "The Politics of Discretion: Federal Intervention in Bilingual Education," *California Law Review, 76*, no. 6 (1988): 1249–1352.
20. James J. Lyons, "The Past and Future Directions of Federal Bilingual-Education Policy," *The Annals of the American Academy of Political and Social Science, 508* (1990): 66–80.
21. T. H Bell, "The Federal Commitment to Bilingual Education," *Annual International Bilingual-Bicultural Education Conference* (San Antonio, TX, 1976).
22. Moran, "The Politics of Discretion."
23. John Molina and Ramon Chavez, "Bilingual Education: A Federal Happening," *NABE, 2*, no. 1 (1978), p. 23.
24. Moran, "The Politics of Discretion."
25. Arnold Leibowitz, *The Bilingual Education Act: A Legislative Analysis* (Arlington: National Clearinghouse for Bilingual Education, 1980).
26. National Advisory Council on Bilingual Education, *Bilingual Education: Quality Education for All Children* (Washington, DC: Office of Bilingual Education, 1975), pp. 14–15.
27. National Advisory Council on Bilingual Education, *Bilingual Education*, p. 15.
28. National Advisory Council on Bilingual Education, *Bilingual Education*, pp. 53–54.
29. Charles R. Foster, "Defusing the Issues in Bilingualism and Bilingual Education," *Phi Delta Kappan, 63*, no. 5 (1982), p. 344.
30. Foster, "Defusing the Issues in Bilingualism and Bilingual Education."
31. Bell, "The Federal Commitment to Bilingual Education," p. 9.
32. Randall Workman, *Bilingual Education: Meeting the Needs of the Eighties* (Washington, DC: National Advisory Council on Bilingual Education, 1983).
33. Betsy Levin, "An Analysis of the Federal Attempt to Regulate Bilingual Education: Protecting Civil Rights or Controlling Curriculum," *Journal of Law & Education, 12*, no. 1 (1983), p. 45.

34. James J. Lyons, "The Past and Future Directions of Federal Bilingual-Education Policy," *The Annals of the American Academy of Political and Social Science, 508* (1990): 66–80.
35. Lori Orum and Raul Yzaguirre, "Secretary Bennett's Bilingual Education Initiative: Historical Perspectives and Implications," *La Raza Law Journal, 1*, no. 3 (1986), p. 231.
36. John O'Connor, "US Social Welfare Policy: The Reagan Record and Legacy," *Journal of Social Policy, 27*, no. 1 (1998): 37–61.
37. Howard Karger and David Stoesz, "Retreat and Retrenchment: Progressives and the Welfare State," *Social Work, 38*, no. 2 (1993): 212–220.
38. Guadalupe San Miguel, Jr., "Bilingual Education Policy Development: The Reagan Years, 1980–1987," *NABE Journal, 12*, no. 2 (1988): 97–112.
39. Orum and Yzaguirre, "Secretary Bennett's Bilingual Education Initiative," p. 247.
40. Orum and Yzaguirre, "Secretary Bennett's Bilingual Education Initiative."
41. Orum and Yzaguirre, "Secretary Bennett's Bilingual Education Initiative," p. 237.
42. Moran, "The Politics of Discretion."
43. Noel Epstein, *Language, Ethnicity and the Schools: Policy Alternatives for Bilingual-Bicultural Education* (Washington, DC: Institute for Educational Leadership, 1977).
44. Robert E. Rossier, "Bilingual Education: Training for the Ghetto," *Policy Review, 25* (Summer 1983), p. 41.
45. Peter Duignan, *Bilingual Education: A Critique* (Stanford, CA: The Hoover Institute on War, Revolution and Peace, 1998), p. 44.
46. Duignan, *Bilingual Education: A Critique*, p. 7.
47. Duignan, *Bilingual Education: A Critique*, p. 37.
48. Duignan, *Bilingual Education: A Critique*, p. 16.
49. Duignan, *Bilingual Education: A Critique*, p. 42.
50. Duignan, *Bilingual Education: A Critique*, p. 37.
51. Duignan, *Bilingual Education: A Critique*, p. 37.
52. Duignan, *Bilingual Education: A Critique*, p. 35.
53. Duignan, *Bilingual Education: A Critique*, p. 46.
54. Duignan, *Bilingual Education: A Critique*, p. 26.
55. Duignan, *Bilingual Education: A Critique*, p. 27.
56. Duignan, *Bilingual Education: A Critique*, p. 27.
57. Glenn Garvin, "Loco, Completamente, Loco," *Reason*, January, 1998, https://reason.com/1998/01/01/loco-completamente-loco/.
58. Garvin, "Loco, Completamente, Loco."
59. Garvin, "Loco, Completamente, Loco."
60. Garvin, "Loco, Completamente, Loco."
61. Garvin, "Loco, Completamente, Loco."
62. James Crawford, *At War with Diversity: US Language Policy in an Age of Anxiety* (Clevedon, UK: Multilingual Matters, 2000), p. 106.
63. Ron Unz, "California and the End of White America," *Commentary* (November 1999), p. 25.
64. Unz, "California and the End of White America," p. 27.

65. Unz, "California and the End of White America," p. 28.
66. Eric Hubler, "Bilingual Ed Ban Fails," *Denver Post*, November 6, 2002.
67. Ron Unz, "Hate Crimes Rising in Colorado," *Ron Unz: Writings and Perspectives*, October 20, 2002. https://www.ronunz.org/2002/10/20/hate-crimes-rising-in-colorado/

Chapter 8

1. Kenneth Clark, *Alternative Public School Systems—A Response to America's Educational Emergency* (Washington, DC: US Commission on Civil Rights, 1967), p. 19.
2. Clark, *Alternative Public School Systems*, p. 22.
3. Bilingual Education Act: Hearings before the General Subcommittee on Education of the Committee on Education and Labor, House of Representatives, 93rd Congress, Washington, DC, 1974, p. 176.
4. Bilingual Education Act: Hearings, p. 176.
5. Bilingual Education Act: Hearings, pp. 177–178.
6. Christian Rivera-Perez, *Aspira Inc. of Illinois: A Tale of Educational Success?* (Capstone Project, Illinois State University, 2007).
7. Aspira's Educational Management Organization, https://aspira.org/about-us/aspiras-educational-management-organization/.
8. Jonathan Kozol, *Free Schools* (Boston: Houghton Mifflin, 1972).
9. K. C. Cole Janssen, *Matters of Choice: A Ford Foundation Report on Alternative Schools* (New York: Ford Foundation, 1974).
10. Stephen Arons, *Alternative Schools: A Practical Manual* (Cambridge, MA: Center for Law and Education at Harvard University, 1971).
11. Milton Friedman, "The Role of Government in Education," in *Economics and the Public Interest*, edited by Robert Solo (New Brunswick, NJ: Rutgers University Press, 1955), 123–144.
12. Christopher Jencks, "Who Should Control Education," *Dissent*, *13*, no. 2 (1966): 145–163.
13. Theodore Sizer, "The Case for a Free Market," *Compact*, *3*, no. 2 (1969), p. 9.
14. Sizer, "The Case for a Free Market," p. 11.
15. Kozol, *Free Schools*, p. 119.
16. Daniel Weiler, *A Public School Voucher Demonstration: The First Year at Alum Rock* (Santa Monica, CA: Rand, 1974).
17. Gail Bass, *A Study of Alternatives in American Education*, Vol. 1: *District Policies and the Implementation of Change* (Santa Monica, CA: RAND, 1978).
18. Nancy Ann Montalvo, *An Evaluation of the Language Center for Limited and Non-English Speaking Students in the Alum Rock Union Elementary School District in San Jose, California* (San Francisco: University of San Francisco, 1980).
19. Oscar Donahue, *Innovations in the Public Schools of Santa Clara County, Spring 1972* (San Jose, CA: Santa Clara County Office, 1972), p. 16.

20. Stephen Weiner and Konrad Kellen, *The Politics and Administration of the Voucher Demonstration in Alum Rock: The First Year, 1972–1973* (Santa Monica, CA: Rand, 1974).
21. Joel Levin, "Educational Alternatives within the Public School System," *Educational Horizons, 52*, no. 1 (1973), p. 31.
22. Levin, "Educational Alternatives within the Public School System," p. 26.
23. Levin, "Educational Alternatives within the Public School System," p. 30.
24. Bass, *A Study of Alternatives in American Education*, Vol. 1, p. 50.
25. Pierce Barker, Tora Bikson, and Jackie Kimbrough, *A Study of Alternatives in American Education*, Vol. V: *Diversity in the Classroom* (Santa Monica, CA: Rand, 1981), p. 15.
26. Levin, "Educational Alternatives within the Public School System," p. 30.
27. Barker, Bikson, and Kimbrough, *A Study of Alternatives in American Education*, Vol. V.
28. C. M. Leinwand Associates, *Educational Voucher Demonstration Archive: Project-Level Documentation* (Newtown: Authors, 1980).
29. Montalvo, *An Evaluation of the Language Center for Limited and Non-English Speaking Students*.
30. Mario Fantini, *Public Schools of Choice* (New York: Simon & Schuster, 1973), p. 39
31. Fantini, *Public Schools of Choice*, p. 247.
32. Etta W. Proshansky, "Choice Not Chance in New York City," *Social Policy, 12*, no. 2 (1981), p. 25.
33. Susan Frelich Appleton, "Alternative Schools for Minority Students: The Constitution, the Civil Rights Act and the Berkeley Experiment," *California Law Review, 61*, no. 3 (1973): 858–918.
34. Larry Wells, "Options in a Small District: Berkeley," *NASSP Bulletin* (September 1973): 55–60.
35. Mary Anne Raywid, "Family Choice Arrangements in Public Schools: A Review of the Literature," *Review of Educational Research, 55*, no. 4 (1985): 435–467.
36. Appleton, "Alternative Schools for Minority Students," p. 858.
37. Southwest Network of the Study Commission on Undergraduate Education and the Education of Teachers, "Preface," in *Chicano Alternative Education* edited by H. Homero Galicia and Clementina Almaguer, (Hayward: Author, 1973), p. iii
38. Clementina Almaguer, "Alternative Chicano Educational Programs in California," in *Chicano Alternative Education* edited by H. Homero Galicia and Clementina Almaguer, (Hayward: Southwest Network of the Study Commission on Undergraduate Education and the Education of Teachers, 1973), 17–28.
39. Southwest Network of the Study Commission on Undergraduate Education and the Education of Teachers, "Interview with Francisco Hernandez, Casa de la Raza Director, Berkeley, CA," in *Chicano Alternative Education* edited by H. Homero Galicia and Clementina Almaguer, (Hayward: Author, 1973), p. 46.
40. Southwest Network of the Study Commission on Undergraduate Education and the Education of Teachers, "Interview with Francisco Hernandez," p. 49.

41. Southwest Network of the Study Commission on Undergraduate Education and the Education of Teachers, "Interview with Francisco Hernandez," p. 49.
42. Southwest Network of the Study Commission on Undergraduate Education and the Education of Teachers, "Interview with Francisco Hernandez," pp. 42–43.
43. Appleton, "Alternative Schools for Minority Students."
44. Appleton, "Alternative Schools for Minority Students."
45. Appleton, "Alternative Schools for Minority Students," p. 898.
46. Appleton, "Alternative Schools for Minority Students," p. 892.
47. Appleton, "Alternative Schools for Minority Students," p. 898.
48. Southwest Network, *Casa de la Raza: Separatism or Segregation?* (Hayward: Authors, 1973).
49. Otha Porter, "Contracted Schools: An Instrument of Educational Change," *The Journal of Negro Education, 40*, no. 3 (1971): 233–239.
50. Ray Budde, *Education by Charter: Restructuring School Districts*, (Andover: Regional Laboratory for Educational Improvement of the Northeast and Islands, 1988).
51. Gary Miron, "Description and Brief History of Charter Schools," in *The Wiley Handbook of School Choice*, edited by Robert Fox and Nina Buchanan (Malden, MA: Wiley-Blackwell, 2017), 224–236.
52. Joe Nathan, "Possibilities, Problems and Progress: Early Lessons from the Charter Movement," *Phi Delta Kappan, 78*, no. 1 (1996), p. 20.
53. Ralph Lieber, "What's to Fear about Charters?" *School Administrator, 54*, no. 7, p. 14.
54. John Collier, "Survival at Rough Rock: A Historical Overview of the Rough Rock," *Anthropology & Education, 19*, no. 3 (1988): 253–269.
55. National Alliance for Public Charter Schools, *Instructional Delivery and Focus of Public Charter Schools: Results from the NAPCS National Charter School Survey* (Washington, DC: Author, 2012), p. 6.
56. Mensah Dean, "Heritage Is Primary Charter School: Emphasizes Bilingual Latino Studies," *The Philadelphia Daily News*, October 23, 1998, p. 6.
57. Dean, "Heritage Is Primary Charter School Emphasizes Bilingual Latino Studies," p. 6.
58. Dean, "Heritage Is Primary Charter School: Emphasizes Bilingual Latino Studies."
59. https://web.archive.org/web/20160324071145/http://www.aspirapa.org/schools-1/.
60. https://web.archive.org/web/20160324071145/http://www.aspirapa.org/schools-1/.
61. Aspira, Inc., of Pennsylvania, *2011 Annual Report: Transforming Our Community through Educational Excellence* (Philadelphia: Author, 2011).
62. Mark Stern and Khuram Hussain, "On the Charter Question: Black Marxism and Black Nationalism," *Race, Ethnicity and Education, 18*, no. 1 (2015): 61–88.
63. Janelle Scott, "The Politics of Venture Philanthropy in Charter School Policy and Advocacy," *Educational Policy, 23*, no. 1 (2009): 106–136.
64. Michael Dumas, "'Waiting for Superman' to Save Black People: Racial Representation and the Official Antiracism of Neoliberal School Reform," *Discourse: Studies in the Cultural Politics of Education, 34*, no. 4 (2013): 531–547.
65. Claudio Sanchez, "Kids Pay the Price in Fight over Fixing Philadelphia Schools," *National Public Radio*, November 21, 2013.

66. Benjamin Herold, "Aspira Wants to Reunite Olney East and West," *Philadelphia Public School Notebook*, May 4, 2011, https://www.chalkbeat.org/philadelphia/2011/5/4/22184335/aspira-wants-to-reunite-olney-east-and-west/.
67. Connie Langland, "Aspira's Excel Program Works to Put Older Students Back on Track," *Philadelphia Public School Notebook*, April 12, 2013, https://www.chalkbeat.org/philadelphia/2013/4/12/22185085/aspira-s-excel-program-works-to-put-older-students-back-on-track/.
68. Bill Hangley, "At Muñoz-Marín, a Contentious Lead-Up to Delayed Renaissance Vote," *Philadelphia Public School Notebook*, June 4, 2014, https://www.chalkbeat.org/philadelphia/2014/6/4/22185736/at-munoz-marin-a-contentious-lead-up-to-delayed-renaissance-vote/.
69. Kevin McCorry, "'Election Season' in North Philly: Parents Hear Pitch on Charter Conversion," *All Things Considered*, April 16, 2014, https://whyy.org/articles/election-season-in-north-philly-parents-hear-pitches-on-charter-conversion/.
70. Hangley, "At Muñoz-Marín, a Contentious Lead-Up." https://www.chalkbeat.org/philadelphia/2014/6/4/22185736/at-munoz-marin-a-contentious-lead-up-to-delayed-renaissance-vote/.
71. Movement Alliance Project, *Revival from the Roots: Tour of Philly's Neighborhood Schools Part 3: Luis Munoz Marin School* (2014), 3:48–4:10.

Chapter 9

1. Joshua Fishman, "The Politics of Bilingual Education," in *Georgetown University Round Table on Languages and Linguistics 1970*, edited by James E. Alatis (Washington, DC: Georgetown University Press, 1970), p. 53.
2. Natalie Gross, "Dual-language Programs on the Rise across the U.S," *Education Writer's Association* August 3, 2016. https://www.ewa.org/blog-latino-ed-beat/dual-language-programs-rise-across-us.
3. www.SealofBiliteracy.org.
4. Michelle Williams, "Como Se Dice? Kindergarten Students at Metcalf in Holyoke Learn Lessons in English and Spanish," *Masslive*, December 22, 2014, https://www.masslive.com/living/2014/12/dual_language_metcalf_holyoke.html.
5. Williams, "Como Se Dice? Kindergarten Students at Metcalf in Holyoke Learn Lessons in English and Spanish."
6. New England Public Media, "Dual Language Education at Holyoke Public Schools," 2:19–2:25. https://www.youtube.com/watch?v=AJdovripCvk
7. New England Public Media, "Dual Language Education at Holyoke Public Schools," 5:07–5:18.
8. Perry Stein, "Are Dual-Language Programs in Urban Schools a Sign of Gentrification?" *Washington Post*, July 3, 2018, https://www.washingtonpost.com/local/education/are-dual-language-programs-in-urban-schools-a-sign-of-gentrification/2018/07/03/926c4a42-68c2-11e8-9e38-24e693b38637_story.html.

9. Stein, "Are Dual-Language Programs in Urban Schools a Sign of Gentrification?" https://www.washingtonpost.com/local/education/are-dual-language-programs-in-urban-schools-a-sign-of-gentrification/2018/07/03/926c4a42-68c2-11e8-9e38-24e693b38637_story.html.
10. John Petrovic, "The Conservative Restoration and the Neoliberal Defense of Bilingual Education," *Language Policy, 4*, no. 4 (2005): 395–416.
11. Mike Mena and Ofelia García, "'Converse Racialization' and 'Un/marking' Language: The Making of a Bilingual University in a Neoliberal World," *Language in Society, 50*, no. 3 (2020): 343–364.
12. Gregory Bourassa, "Neoliberal Multiculturalism and Productive Inclusion: Beyond the Politics of Fulfillment in Education," *Journal of Education Policy, 36*, no. 2 (2021): 253–278.
13. Wayne Thomas and Virginia Collier, "Dual Language Education for All," in *Dual Language Education: Teaching and Leading in Two Languages*, edited by David DeMatthews and Elena Izquierdo (Cham: Springer, 2019), 91–105.
14. Noah Katznelson and Katie Bernstein, "Rebranding Bilingualism: The Shifting Discourses of Language Education Policy in California's 2016 Election," *Linguistics and Education, 40* (2017): 11–26.
15. *English Proficiency: Multilingual Education Initiative Statute, California Proposition 58* (2016), p. 146.
16. *English Proficiency: Multilingual Education Initiative Statute, California Proposition 58* (2016), p. 146
17. *English Proficiency: Multilingual Education Initiative Statute, California Proposition 58* (2016), p. 146.
18. *English Proficiency: Multilingual Education Initiative Statute, California Proposition 58* (2016), p. 146.
19. *English Proficiency: Multilingual Education Initiative Statute, California Proposition 58* (2016), p. 146.
20. *English Proficiency: Multilingual Education Initiative Statute, California Proposition 58* (2016), p. 146.
21. *English Proficiency: Multilingual Education Initiative Statute, California Proposition 58* (2016), p. 146.
22. *English Proficiency: Multilingual Education Initiative Statute, California Proposition 58* (2016), p. 146.
23. Nelson Flores and Jonathan Rosa, "Undoing Appropriateness: Raciolinguistic Ideologies and Language Diversity in Education," *Harvard Educational Review, 85*, no. 2 (2015): 149–171.
24. Laura Chávez-Moreno, "Dual Language as White Property: Examining a Secondary Bilingual-Education Program and Latinx Equity," *American Educational Research Journal, 58*, no. 6 (2021): 1107–1141.
25. Verónica Valdez, Juan Freire, and M. Garrett Delavan, "The Gentrification of Dual Language Education," *The Urban Review, 48*, no. 4 (2016): 601–627.
26. Because some of the anecdotes presented here were collected as part of an IRB-approved study that I undertook, pseudonyms are used for both schools.

27. I developed a working relationship with Washington Elementary school in partnership with my former doctoral student Sofia Chaparro, who ended up doing her dissertation research at the school. You can read more about the family dynamics that I am describing here in one of the articles that she published based on her dissertation research: Sofia Chaparro, "School, Parents and Communities: Leading Parallel Lives in a Two-Way Immersion Program," *International Multilingual Research Journal, 14*, no. 1 (2020): 41–57.
28. You can find out more about Hamilton Elementary School and other schools in the same neighborhood that confronted similar challenges in an article I published with a former graduate student: Nelson Flores and Lauren McAuliff, "'In Other Schools You Can Plan It That Way': A Raciolinguistic Perspective on Dual Language Education," *International Journal of Bilingual Education and Bilingualism, 25*, no. 4 (2022):1349–1362.
29. The term "The Badlands" was first used in this novel: Steven Lopez, *Third and Indiana* (New York: Penguin Books, 1994). It has since become widely used, including on Google maps: Patricia Madej, "'Philadelphia Badlands' Label in Google Maps Latest Controversy over Neighborhood Names," *Philadelphia Inquirer*, May 2, 2019, https://www.inquirer.com/news/philadelphia/philadelphia-badlands-google-maps-neighborhood-names-20190502.html.
30. Corey Mitchell, "'English-Only' Laws in Education on Verge of Extinction," *Education Week*, October 23, 2019, https://www.edweek.org/teaching-learning/english-only-laws-in-education-on-verge-of-extinction/2019/10.
31. Claudia Cervantes-Soon, James Gambrell, G. Sue Kasun, Wenyang Sun, Juan Freire, and Lisa Dorner, "'Everybody Wants a Choice' in Dual Language Education of El Nuevo Sur: Whiteness as the Gloss for Everybody in Media Discourses of Multilingual Education," *Journal of Language, Identity and Education, 20*, no. 6 (2021): 394–410.
32. Valdez, Freire, and Delavan, "The Gentrification of Dual Language Education," p. 613.
33. Lisa Dorner, Jeong-Mi Moon, Edwin Nii Bonney, and Alexandria Otis, "Dueling Discourses in Dual Language Schools: Multilingual 'Success for All' versus the Academic 'Decline' of Black Students," in *Bilingualism for All? Raciolinguistic Perspectives on Dual Language Education in the United States*, edited by Nelson Flores, Amelia Tseng, and Nicholas Subtirelu (Clevedon, UK: Multilingual Matters, 2020), 88–110.

Chapter 10

1. Nelson Flores, "A Tale of Two Visions: Hegemonic Whiteness and Bilingual Education," *Educational Policy, 30*, no. 1 (2016): 13–38.
2. Judith Butler, *Bodies That Matter: On the Discursive Limits of "Sex"* (New York: Routledge, 1993).
3. Yolanda Sealey-Ruiz, "The Critical Literacy of Race: Toward Racial Literacy in Urban Teacher Education," in *Handbook of Urban Education*, edited by H. Richard Milner and Kofi Lomotey (New York: Routledge, 2021): 281–295.

4. Ofelia García, Nelson Flores, Kate Seltzer, Li Wei, Ricardo Otheguy, and Jonathan Rosa, "Rejecting Abyssal Thinking in the Language and Education of Racialized Bilinguals: A Manifesto," *Critical Inquiry in Language Studies, 18*, no. 3 (2021): 203–228.
5. Walter Mignolo, *The Idea of Latin America* (Malden, MA: Blackwell, 2006).
6. Laura Gomez, "Opposite 'One-Drop Rule,' Mexican Americans, African Americans and the Need to Reconceive Turn of the Twentieth Century Race Relations," in *How the United States Racializes Latinos*, edited by José Cobas, Jorge Duany, and Joe Feagin (New York: Routledge, 2009), 87–100.
7. George A. Martinez, "The Legal Construction of Race: Mexican-Americans and Whiteness," *Harvard Latino Law Review, 2* (1997): 321–348.
8. Rubén Donato and Jarrod Hanson, "Mexican-American Resistance to School Segregation," *Phi Delta Kappan, 100*, no. 5 (2019): 39–42.
9. Pedro Caban, "The Colonizing Mission of the U.S. in Puerto Rico," in *Transnational Latino/a Communities: Re-examining Politics, Processes and Culture*, edited by Carlos Vélez-Ibañez and A. Sampaio (Lanham, MD: Rowman and Littlefield, 2002), p. 115–145.
10. Déborah Berman Santana, "Puerto Rico's Operation Bootstrap: Colonial Roots of a Persistent Model for 'Third World' Development," *Revista Geográfica, 124* (1998): 87–116.
11. Kenzo K. Sung and Ayana Allen-Hardy, "Contradictory Origins and Racializing Legacy of the 1968 Bilingual Education Act: Urban Schooling, Anti-Blackness, and Oakland's 1996 Black English Language Education Policy," *University of Maryland Law Journal of Race, Religion, Gender and Class, 19*, no. 1 (2019): 44–80.
12. Evelyn Bauer, "Bilingual Education in BEA Schools," *TESOL Quarterly, 4*, no. 3 (1970): 223–229.
13. Flores, "A Tale of Two Visions."
14. Ronn Pineo, *Ecuador and the United States: Useful Strangers* (Athens: University of Georgia Press, 2010).
15. Brad D. Jokisch, "From Labor Circulation to International Migration: The Case of South-Central Ecuador," *Yearbook, Conference of Latin Americanist Geographers, 23* (1997): 63–75.
16. Juan Gonzalez, *Harvest of Empire: A History of Latinos in America* (New York: Penguin Books, 2011).
17. Christopher Busey and Carolyn Silva, "Troubling the Essentialist Discourse of *Brown* in Education: The Anti-Black Sociopolitical and Sociohistorical Etymology of Latinxs as a *Brown* Monolith," *Educational Researcher, 50*, no. 3 (2020): 176–186; Luis Urrieta and Dolores Calderón, "Critical Latinx Indigeneities: Unpacking Indigeneity from Within and Outside of Latinized Entanglements," *Association of Mexican American Educators Journal, 13*, no. 2 (2019): 145–174.
18. Sofia Chaparro, " 'But Mom! I'm Not a Spanish Boy': Raciolinguistic Socialization in a Two-Way Immersion Bilingual Program," *Linguistics and Education, 50* (2019): 1–12.
19. Jonathan Rosa, "Standardization, Racialization, Languagelessness: Raciolinguistic Ideologies across Communicative Contexts," *Journal of Linguistic Anthropology, 26*, no. 2 (2016): 162–183.

20. Eva Midobuch, "From LEP to Academic: Reflections on My Twenty Years in Title VII," *Bilingual Research Journal, 22*, no. 1 (1998): 49–63.
21. Jim Cummins, *Language, Power and Pedagogy: Bilingual Children in the Crossfire* (Clevedon, UK: Multilingual Matters, 2000).
22. Virginia Collier and Wayne Thomas, "The Astounding Effectiveness of Dual Language Education for All," *NABE Journal of Research and Practice, 2*, no. 1 (2004): 1–20.
23. Ofelia García, "Unblocking *Tapones* and Finding Pleasant Places," *Education Review, 28* (2021): 1–14.
24. Ofelia García, *Bilingual Education in the 21st Century: A Global Perspective* (Malden, MA: Wiley-Blackwell, 2009).
25. García et al., "Rejecting Abyssal Thinking in the Language and Education of Racialized Bilingual Students."
26. Nelson Flores and Jonathan Rosa, "Undoing Appropriateness: Raciolinguistic Ideologies and Language Diversity in Education," *Harvard Educational Review, 85*, no. 2 (2015): 149–171.
27. Jonathan Rosa and Nelson Flores, "Unsettling Race and Language: Toward a Raciolinguistic Perspective," *Language in Society, 46*, no. 5 (2017): 621–647.
28. Nelson Flores and Jonathan Rosa, "Undoing Competence: Coloniality, Homogeneity, and the Overrepresentation of Whiteness in Applied Linguistics," *Language Learning* (2023): 268–295.
29. One prominent example here is Jim Cummins, "Teaching Minoritized Students: Are Additive Approaches Legitimate?" *Harvard Educational Review, 87*, no. 3: 404–425.
30. One prominent example here is Guadalupe Valdés, "Analyzing the Curricularization of Language in Two-Way Immersion Education: Restating Two Cautionary Notes," *Bilingual Research Journal, 41*, no. 4 (2018): 388–412.

Index

For the benefit of digital users, indexed terms that span two pages (e.g., 52–53) may, on occasion, appear on only one of those pages.